RICHARD WAGNER
AND
FESTIVAL THEATRE

RICHARD WAGNER
AND
FESTIVAL THEATRE

SIMON WILLIAMS

Contributions in Drama and Theatre Studies, Number 53

LIVES OF THE THEATRE

JOSH BEER and CHRISTOPHER INNES, Series Advisers

Greenwood Press
Westport, Connecticut • London

Library of Congress Cataloging-in-Publication Data

Williams, Simon.
    Richard Wagner and festival theatre / Simon Williams.
       p. cm.—(Contributions in drama and theatre studies, ISSN
  0163–3821 ; no. 53) (Lives of the theatre)
    Includes bibliographical references and index.
    ISBN 0–313–27435–5 (alk. paper).
    1. Wagner, Richard, 1813–1883. 2. Wagner, Richard, 1813–1883—
Performances—Germany—Bayreuth. 3. Festspielhaus (Bayreuth,
Germany). I. Series. II. Series: Lives of the theatre.
ML410.W13W43   1994
782.1′092—dc20   93–34081

British Library Cataloguing in Publication Data is available.

A paperback edition of *Richard Wagner and Festival Theatre* is available
from the Praeger Publishers imprint of Greenwood Publishing Group, Inc.
(ISBN: 0–275–93608–2).

Library of Congress Catalog Card Number: 93–34081
ISBN: 0–313–27435–5
ISSN: 0163–3821

First published in 1994

Greenwood Press, 88 Post Road West, Westport, CT 06881
An imprint of Greenwood Publishing Group, Inc.

Printed in the United States of America

∞™

The paper used in this book complies with the
Permanent Paper Standard issued by the National
Information Standards Organization (Z39.48–1984).

10 9 8 7 6 5 4 3 2 1

For
"Little One"

Contents

Illustrations

Series Foreword

Lives of the Theatre is designed to provide scholarly introductions to important periods and movements in the history of world theatre from the earliest instances of recorded performance through to the twentieth century, viewing the theatre consistently through the lives of representative theatrical practitioners. Although many of the volumes will be centered upon playwrights, other important theatre people, such as actors and directors, will also be prominent in the series. The subjects have been chosen not simply for their individual importance, but because their lives in the theatre can well serve to provide a major perspective on the theatrical trends of their eras. They are therefore either representative of their time, figures whom their contemporaries recognized as vital presences in the theatre, or they are people whose work had a fundamental influence on the development of theatre, not only in their lifetimes but after their deaths as well. While the discussion of verbal and written scripts will inevitably be a central concern in any volume that is about an artist who wrote for the theatre, these scripts will always be considered in their function as a basis for performance.

The rubric "Lives of the Theatre" is therefore intended to suggest biographies both of people who created theatre as an institution and as a medium of performance and of the life of the theatre itself. This dual focus will be illustrated through the titles of the individual volumes, such as *Christopher Marlowe and the Renaissance of Tragedy*, *George Bernard Shaw and the Socialist Theatre*, and *Richard Wagner and Festival Theatre*, to name just a few. At the same time, although the focus of each volume will be different, depending on the particular subject, appropriate emphasis will be given to the cultural and political context within which the theatre of any given time is set. Theatre itself can be seen to have a palpable effect upon the social world around it, as it both reflects the life of its time and helps to form that life by feeding it images, epitomes, and alternative versions of itself. Hence, we hope that this series will also contribute to understanding the broader social life of the period of which the theatre represented in each volume was a part.

Lives of the Theatre grew out of an idea that Josh Beer put to Christopher Innes and Peter Arnott. Sadly, Peter did not live to see the inauguration of the series. Simon Williams kindly agreed to replace him as one of the series' editors and has played a full part in its preparation. In commemoration, the editors wish to acknowledge Peter's own rich contribution to the life of the theatre.

Josh Beer
Christopher Innes

Preface

While this book was in the process of completion, six new publications on Richard Wagner appeared: two large edited collections on his whole life and output, one edited collection on his music dramas in performance, a polemical treatment of his anti-Semitism, and two discussions of his theoretical writings. Such an abundance of new writings had led me to pay even greater attention than usual to answering the question that proverbially faces all authors on Wagner—why write yet another book on a seemingly exhausted topic?

Perhaps the most obvious answer is that any great artist's works are inexhaustible and therefore constantly in need of discussion. But Richard Wagner offers a particular fascination. He was such a protean figure that there are few spheres of artistic and intellectual activity in the nineteenth or indeed the twentieth centuries upon which his work did not eventually have some influence. It is, of course, as a composer that he is best known to history, but it can well be argued that his career as a theatrical reformer was no less significant.

Wagner as a theatre practitioner provides the unifying and, I hope, distinguishing theme of the present biography. In fact, this has not always been an easy theme to pursue. While Wagner considered himself skilled equally in the arts of the dramatist and the composer, to the degree that he often understood these two vocations as identical, posterity is perhaps right in thinking of him primarily as a composer. It was to music that he owed his ultimate and unquestioning loyalty, while his attitude to the theatre was ambivalent in the extreme. He hated it, and yet he could not do without it.

The hatred grew from his awareness of how far the theatre of his time was from the ideal that he knew it could achieve, and the need from a temperament that constantly drove him to express himself in theatrical terms. The personal crises associated with his dealings with the theatre arose consistently from his uncompromising determination that theatre should be capable of expressing his artistic vision to the fullest. The dilemma he faced was not, of course, exclusive to him, as theatre artists for centuries have been forced to work within an institution that, more often than not, may be unsympathetic to their ambitions. Few, however, have gone so far to remedy the situation as Wagner did.

In so doing, he prepared the ground for transformations in the social function of theatre that fully occurred only in the twentieth century. Throughout Wagner's lifetime, the prime functions of theatre, both operatic and spoken, were to provide mass entertainment and to offer a locus in which society could display itself to itself. Wagner, by insisting on artistic integrity and wholeness in stage performance and on the primacy of that performance in the theatrical event, was unusual for his time. His elevation of performance provided the theatre with unwonted vitality. Since his death, several preeminent stage directors and the theatres within which they work have been inspired by a vision of the potential of theatre to energize and alter society. This vision can be traced back to him. Therefore, while Wagner is usually considered within the context of music history, his role in the history of the theatre is of equal importance.

Since the focus of this study is on Wagner as a man of the theatre, the principal documents to be studied include his extensive writings on the theatre, while the principal events are those that led up to the crowning achievements of his career—the building of the Bayreuth Festival Theatre and the founding of the Bayreuth Festival. The great music dramas are, however, equally central to a study of Wagner in the theatre, both because they remain central to the operatic repertoire to this day and because the dramas and the theatre in which they were to be performed ultimately came to be fused in Wagner's mind. Hence, this biography includes critical and dramaturgical analyses of all of Wagner's major and minor works for the stage.

I would like to acknowledge the support of the Research Committee of the Academic Senate of the University of California, Santa Barbara, for their grant of funds that allowed me to travel to Germany to attend a number of Wagner productions and to visit relevant museums and archives. Some of my material on the Bayreuth Theatre has already appeared in my article "Bayreuth *Festspielhaus*: Enchaining the Audience," published in *Theatre Survey* 33: 1 (May 1992): 65–73. It is republished here with the kind permission of the editor. Thanks are due to Sandy Hortmann and Maik Hamburger for their hospitality and aid while I was in Germany, to Martin Silver of the Music Library at UCSB for his help in matters relating to Wagner bibliography, and to Peter Mark who kindly read the complete manuscript.

Abbreviations

BaRW. Oswald Georg Bauer. *The Stage Designs and Productions from the Premières to the Present Day.*

BeRW. Paul Bekker. *Richard Wagner.*

CWD. Cosima Wagner. *Diaries.*

GSB. Richard Wagner. *Gesammelte Schriften und Briefe.*

HBEY. Robert Hartford. *Bayreuth: The Early Years.*

LuWB. Otto Strabel, ed. *König Ludwig und Richard Wagner Briefwechsel.*

ML. Richard Wagner. *Mein Leben.*

NLRW. Ernest Newman. *The Life of Richard Wagner.*

NUM. Friedrich Nietzsche. *Untimely Meditations.*

NWC. *Nietzsche-Wagner Correspondence.*

NWO. Ernest Newman. *The Wagner Operas.*

PWRR. Heinrich Porges. *Wagner Rehearses the Ring.*

RWMWa. *Richard Wagner an Minna Wagner.*

RWMW. *Richard Wagner an Mathilde Wesendonk.*

RWFZ. *Richard Wagner an Freunde und Zeitgenossen.*

RWSA. Jack Stein. *Richard Wagner and the Synthesis of the Arts.*

SB. Richard Wagner. *Sämtliche Briefe.*

TWC. Michael Tanner, "The Total Work of Art," *The Wagner Companion.*

WLB. *Wagner-Liszt Briefwechsel.*

Chapter 1

The Fiery Conformist

From the day of his birth, 22 May 1813, Richard Wagner would seem to have been destined for a life in the theatre. His father, Carl Friedrich Wagner, an actuary with the Leipzig police, was a skilled amateur actor; the writer E.T.A. Hoffmann met him once in a tavern and found him "an exotic character . . . an adherent of the better school [of acting], *un poco exaltato* after imbibing a lot of rum."[1] The elder Wagner died a mere six months after Richard's birth in a typhus epidemic that broke out after the defeat of Napoleon at the battle of Leipzig. Soon after, his wife, Johanna, married Ludwig Geyer, a close family friend who may have been Richard's natural father. Geyer was a professional artist of all trades: a portrait painter, an actor, a singer, and a playwright. His most successful piece, *Der Bethlehemische Kindermord* (*The Massacre of the Innocents*, 1821), despite its title a comedy about an artist's marriage, was quite widely performed in its day and even praised by Johann Wolfgang von Goethe. While Johanna was indifferent to theatre, her children were not. Her eldest son, Albert, became a singer, and three of her five daughters, prior to their marriages, made respectable careers as actresses or opera singers. Not surprisingly, Richard, the youngest of Johanna's three sons, gravitated toward the theatre for his livelihood as well.

From his mother's and Geyer's marriage in August 1814 until the latter's death in September 1821, Richard lived in close association with the actors and musicians of the Dresden Court Theatre where his stepfather was employed. When he was three years old, he even appeared on stage in a festive play celebrating the return of the King of Saxony to his capital after his imprisonment following the Napoleonic wars; young Richard played an angel "sewn up in tights and with wings on my back, in a graceful pose which I had learnt with difficulty."[2] More memorably, just before his seventh birthday, Richard played the younger son of Wilhelm Tell in Friedrich von Schiller's tragedy, with his sister Clara as Walther, Tell's elder son. As Clara left the stage in the company of her "father," Richard, presciently confusing illusion with reality, insisted on following her rather than remaining on stage with the actress playing his "mother." Geyer, who had little confidence in his stepson's mimetic abilities, acknowledged that this showed some talent for improvisation.

Theatrical performances were part of the Geyer family life as well. Geyer wrote plays to celebate special occasions, and Richard remembered acting the role of a street urchin in a private presentation of Franz Grillparzer's *Sappho*. Like many children of his age, he developed a taste for puppet theatres and even staged Carl Maria von Weber's *Der Freischütz*, which had deeply moved him when he saw it in the opera house. But his compelling attachment to theatre arose neither from sheer delight at the illusion it offered nor from a superficial desire for entertainment. Rather, theatre seemed literally to seduce him. He was a delicate child; in fact, when he was very young, it was uncertain whether he would survive childhood. He possessed a correspondingly sensitive and even morbid imagination that disturbingly populated the inanimate world around him. When exercised on the gloomy rooms of the houses where he lived, such imaginative projections could terrify him. In the theatre, by contrast, these imaginings gratified him. Backstage he claimed to experience "the exciting pleasure at being in an environment that was entirely different from that of everyday life, a world that was purely fantastic and often dreadfully attractive" (*ML*, 1, 17). This sensation acquired erotic dimensions when he touched costumes, especially those worn by his sisters, for they "exercised a subtly exciting effect on my fantasy; merely touching them could make my heart beat wildly" (*ML*, 1, 18). As he grew older, theatre increasingly represented the pleasurable opposite of what he experienced as the oppression of everyday life.

In the early nineteenth century, theatre was rising in the esteem of the German public as an institution that cultivated citizens, but it was still largely beyond the pale of respectability for an individual to earn a living in it.[3] Despite some improvement in public esteem for actors and in levels of compensation, the theatre was still mainly a haven for the failed professional or man of letters and for the underprivileged of the middle classes, rather than an occupation that people willingly followed. Richard's father had, exceptionally, encouraged his children to take up theatre, but Geyer, before he died, urged Johanna to prevent Richard from following in his footsteps. Instead, he hoped that Richard would acquire an education to prepare him for a more acceptable profession. As a result, in December 1822, Richard was enrolled in the Dresden Kreuzschule, where he remained until December 1827.

At school, Richard's hyperactive imagination stood in the way of his procuring a thorough training in any discipline. Incapable of systematic study, he would follow his enthusiasms and, without preparation, would plunge into whatever fascinated him, reading far beyond the level of knowledge expected of the beginner. When he discovered that he could not pursue his interests as far as he wished, he would retrace his steps in order to master the preliminaries but only so that he could return as soon as possible to his advanced reading. For example, he became fascinated with Greek mythology but achieved little in the field because he learned Greek unmethodically and so his knowledge of mythology was always rudimentary. The same impulsive habits marked his apprenticeships in drama and music, bringing upon him charges of dilettantism that would stick throughout his life. Nevertheless, his time at the Kreuzschule was not wasted. His intelligence and capacity for hard work, however unsystematic, meant that he advanced regularly. In particular, he displayed a talent for poetry that was publicly recognized when he was awarded a prize for a commemorative poem on the sudden death of a fellow pupil. But his main literary achievement at this time was the composition of "a stupendous tragic play," a secret undertaking that took him two years to complete.

Among the oddest offspring of the German passion for William Shakespeare, the young Wagner's *Leubald and Adelaide* is known less for its inherent qualities than for the description Wagner wrote of it in an "Autobiographical Sketch" that he published fifteen or so years later:

> I drew up a great tragedy, which was almost a compilation of *Hamlet* and *King Lear*. The plan was extremely grandiose. Forty-two people died in the course of the piece and to complete the action I saw myself obliged to have most of them return as ghosts, because otherwise I would have run out of characters in the last act.[4]

In actuality, the play was not so spectacularly absurd. The action as described in a surviving outline (*GSB*, VI, 7–14) is gory enough, as the hero Leubald slaughters the whole clan that killed his father, only to fall deliriously in love with his final victim, Adelaide. A mere twenty-one characters are involved in this farrago, and, since a fair number of them survive to the final act, multiple spectral visitations are unnecessary. The character types and the love-death of Leubald and Adelaide prefigure the later *Tristan and Isolde*, but equally significant is the magnified utterance and extremity of emotion that would eventually be among the strongest attributes of Wagner's mature work. As one of his earliest biographers put it, "in this Tragedy, the Tragic is hyper-tragic, the Comic is ultra-comic, the Grotesque super-grostesque, [and] the Coarse out-henry-the-eighths Henry the Eighth."[5]

Wagner did not continue to cultivate his purely dramatic talent, partly because his family was distressed by his very act of writing a play, but, more consequentially, because he felt that words alone were inadequate to express the tumultuous experience he wished to articulate. Music, he sensed, offered a more appropriate dramatic language. For most of his life, drama and music occupied his attention equally, as if they were identical phenomena, but the understanding that he would be a composer as well as a dramatist seems to have dawned on him only after he left Dresden at the end of 1827. He then moved to join his family in Leipzig where his sister Rosalie had been appointed actress at the Court Theatre. Since he was still only fourteen, his education continued at the Leipzig Nikolaischule, where his interest in academic subjects waned as his affinity to music grew.

Wagner is unusual among major composers, in that his proclivity toward music did not manifest itself until late in adolescence. Although as a child he had had occasional piano lessons, he was considered to be the least musical member of his family. He was not ignorant of music, however. Both Weber, director of German opera at the Dresden Court Theatre, and the castrato Sassaroli, director of Italian opera, had been frequent visitors to his house when he was a child. His later preference for German over Italian opera may have originated in his intense dislike of the Italian's high-pitched voice and rolls of quivering flesh; a more positive cause may have been his idolization of Weber's *Der Freischütz*, the first work to give German music and theatre its own identity after the Napoleonic wars. The concerts he heard in Dresden seemed to have affected him much as theatre had in his early childhood, appealing primarily as sensuous experiences. In his autobiography, he recalled: "the enchanting pleasure I felt at hearing an orchestra play very close to me is still one of my more pleasant memories" (*ML*, 1, 39).

It was only after sensing the need for music in *Leubald* and some decisive experiences in Leipzig that music became his major passion. With Rosalie engaged at the Court Theatre, his name was on the free list, so he attended performances regularly, acquainting himself with the classical repertoire of Schiller and Shakespeare and the operas of Heinrich

Marschner and Weber. One especially memorable experience occurred during the visit of the dramatic soprano Wilhelmine Schröder-Devrient to sing the lead in Ludwig van Beethoven's *Fidelio*, an event that he claimed changed his life: "Whoever remembers this wonderful woman at that period of her life must in some way be able to confirm the almost demonic ardor that flowed over him with the human and ecstatic art of this incomprable actress" (*ML*, 1, 50). The accuracy of his memory has been questioned,[6] but the conception of the artist as a purveyor of energy to the audience, rather than as a pure technician or paragon of deportment, was fundamental to his later vision of the function of music and theatre in society. What is certain is that during his adolescent years in Leipzig, he developed a profound enthusiasm for Beethoven's music, including later, difficult works such as the Choral Symphony (the ninth), which, due to the inadequacies of contemporary orchestral playing, were beyond the comprehension of both musicians and their public. Wagner, however, soon placed Beethoven beside Shakespeare as the creative genius he most emulated, a twin standing that would remain unchanged until his death.

A temperament as active as Wagner's was not content merely to absorb music but needed music to express itself. Even here, however, Wagner was incapable of systematic study. He first attempted to acquire the rudiments of music from a standard text book, but this undertaking achieved nothing more than a hefty library fine when he failed to return the book on time—the first of countless debts that would encumber him all his life. Then, secretly, since his family was still averse to an artistic career, he took lessons with a violinist in the Leipzig Gewandhaus Orchestra; again, he made little progress. Only in 1831, after enrolling at Leipzig University, did he encounter a teacher whom he trusted, Christian Theodor Weinlig, cantor at the Thomaskirche. Fittingly for a man who occupied the position once held by Johann Sebastian Bach, Weinlig was the most noted contrapuntist of his age, and the six months he spent instructing Wagner in counterpoint left an indelible mark on the latter's future composition. Weinlig's recognition of the young man's talents as a composer and his refusal to accept payment for the lessons did much to reconcile Johanna Wagner to her son's future career in the arts, which was now becoming an accepted fact in the family.

Despite his lack of formal training, Wagner did not hesitate to compose prolifically. The majority of his early work—sonatas, concert overtures, a string quartet, songs, and incidental music for the theatre—was not performed and has been lost. His debut as a composer, at a concert in the Leipzig Court Theatre on 25 December 1830, was far from auspicious. The piece in question, an "Overture in B flat" (subsequently lost), featured an insistent drumbeat once every four bars; this became so predictable that the audience was reduced to laughter, and the young composer slunk shamefacedly from the chamber. Yet on this as on so many future occasions, he was able to resort to his rich imagination to shield him from hostility or contempt. At the Christmas concert the following year, another overture, which has survived, was given a more sympathetic hearing. In 1832, the good offices of Weinlig led to the publication of some of Wagner's piano music. Another concert overture was performed in Leipzig in March of that year, and the following November his only symphony was played in Prague. To his contemporaries, Wagner seemed a talented though unoriginal composer, clearly indebted to Beethoven.

Despite his growing preoccupation with music, Wagner never lost his love of theatre nor the propensity to express himself in stridently theatrical gestures. For example, he enrolled in Leipzig University mainly because he was fascinated by the flamboyant colors favored by fraternities, such as the Saxonia Club. During this late adolescent phase, he engaged in disconcertingly violent activities. During the July Revolution of 1830, he joined in riots, which included tearing down a popular brothel, and, as a member of the Saxonia Club, he escaped serious injury, perhaps even death, only when the opponent he was due to fight was killed in an earlier duel. He also gambled recklessly.

Fortunately, his energies soon found more productive channels. Wagner dissociated himself from his student colleagues when he discovered that they were indifferent to political matters and, in the summer of 1832, he expanded his horizons by visiting Vienna, a city whose pleasures he appreciated but whose musical and theatrical life struck him as superficial. Soon after his return, at a performance of his symphony at the Leipzig Gewandhaus, he met Heinrich Laube, the most prominent member of the loosely affiliated group of writers known as *Junges Deutschland* (Young Germany). This group advocated a more just society that would allow, among other things, greater sexual freedom. At this time, Wagner completed the libretto of a work he intended to be his first opera, *Die Hochzeit (The Marriage)*, another turbulent piece about interclan warfare set in the Middle Ages. The action of this piece reaches its climax when the hero, who is attending a wedding, is flung to his death from a balcony by the bride whom he has attempted to rape. The subsequent mystifying expiration of the bride on the coffin of her assailant is another lurid foreshadowing of the love-death of *Tristan and Isolde*. Wagner started on the score—a skillfully constructed septet has survived—but abandoned work when his sister Rosalie, his mentor in artistic matters, objected to the opera's gratuitous violence.

Soon after, in January 1833, his brother Albert secured him an appointment as chorus master at the Würzburg theatre. This first professional
contact with the theatre resulted, characteristically as it would turn out, in
markedly ambivalent feelings. On the one hand, young Wagner gained
invaluable experience through training the chorus in the standard works
of the operatic repertoire; on the other, he found the routine wearing. He
was particularly irked by having to work with what he considered inferior
material, especially the major new production of the season, Giacomo
Meyerbeer's *Robert le Diable* (*Robert the Devil*). For all the opera's
celebrity, Wagner found it "transparent," and daily contact with it led to
his "aesthetic demoralization" (*ML*, 1, 101). For the first and far from the
last time, his musical and dramatic sense did not allow him to accept a
work whose sole purpose, he claimed, was to please the public.

The Würzburg episode was far from unproductive, however. Wagner's
duties in the threatre ended in April, but he remained in the city for the
rest of the year, working on the score of his first completed opera, *Die
Feen* (*The Fairies*). This work had no impact on the history of the theatre,
since it was not performed until 1888, some five years after Wagner's
death, but it is still of interest, both for some passages of attractive music
and because it demonstrates how the work of the future operatic revolutionary was firmly based in the popular romantic theatre. The most
frequently performed German-language operas of the time were by Carl
Maria von Weber (1786–1826) and Marschner (1795–1861), who drew
their material from German folkore and legend. In Weber's *Der Freischütz*
(*The Freeshooter*, 1821) and Marschner's *Der Vampyr* (*The Vampire*,
1828), the gothic environment and supernatural atmosphere serve as
metaphors for the darker, destructive aspects of the human psyche. The
music not only articulates the emotional life of the dramatic characters,
but also, in extended passages such as the celebrated Wolf's Glen scene
in *Der Freischütz*, conjures up disturbing realms in which the supernatural
threatens the stabilitiy of the fragile human world. Less gloomy were the
spectacular fairy-plays by the Viennese actor and dramatist Ferdinand
Raimund (1790–1836), whose work had offered Wagner his only satisfying theatrical experience during his visit to Vienna in 1832. In Raimund's
comedies such as *Der Bauer als Millionär* (*The Peasant as Millionaire*,
1826) and *Der Alpenkönig und der Menschenfeind* (*The Alpine King and
the Misanthrope*, 1828), then widely performed in German-speaking
Europe, the supernatural has a more benign and nurturing influence upon
human life, leading to the reconciliation of lovers and the unification of
families. This mode of theatre could exercise an unusually pleasurable
appeal. It reached its apogee in Berlin in 1843, when Ludwig Tieck, the

éminence grise of German letters whose career sketched back to the earliest days of Romanticism, staged the first German production of *A Midsummer Night's Dream* with the famous music by Felix Mendelssohn.

The Fairies is based on *La donna serpente* (*The Snake Woman*, 1762) by the Italian playwright Carlo Gozzi (1720–1806), whose work was enjoying a considerable vogue in Germany at that time, serving too as a model for Raimund and other popular dramatists. In *The Fairies*, a human prince, Arindal, has married a fairy, Ada, but can stay with her only if, for eight years, he does not ask her who she is. Not surprisingly, he cannot do this and is forced to return to the human world. Ada follows him, putting his love for her through intolerable trials. When he fails these tests and curses her, she is turned to stone. She returns to her fairy state only when Arindal, Orpheus-like, breaks the spell that binds her through the beauty of his song. The opera ends with the reconciled pair renouncing the world for eternal life as fairies.

A unique feature of *The Fairies* was that the libretto and music were written by the same person. This offended Laube, who had offered to write libretti for Wagner, but Wagner, who aspired to total control over his artistic works, insisted on this practice throughout his career. Dramatically, *The Fairies* is unmistakably an apprentice work. While the plot is concentrated, it is far from coherent, and, despite lengthy passages of exposition (a continuing problem even in Wagner's later stage works), the audience can be as much in the dark as the characters are as to what is going on. Furthermore, while the intermingling of the supernatural and human spheres is minutely observed, the separate levels of action are poorly integrated. In particular, a pair of comic lovers, intended as a foil for two pairs of serious fairy and human lovers, are awkwardly grafted onto the action; while their duet, which sounds at times like a parody of Beethoven's Leonora and Florestan, is full of life and wit, dramatically it is heavy-handed. Above all, the action is driven by no necessity, so that characteristic stage effects of the Romantic theatre, such as elaborate disguises or Ada's test of Arindal's love by seeming to hurl their children into a flaming abyss, strike the viewer as gratuitous.

In contrast, the music is surprisingly accomplished for so young a composer. Weber and Marschner were his primary models, and one can hear harmonic patterns reminiscent of Mendelssohn's overture to *A Midsummer Night's Dream* (1826). Nonetheless, the music does not always articulate the drama effectively. It evokes an enchanting and magical environment, but, since the characters are rarely more than ciphers, the music remains descriptive and can rarely be used as a dramatic medium. Exceptions to this are passages for Ada and Arindal; an opening recitative and aria for Arindal forcefully represent his desolation and panic, while his madness in act 3 foreshadows the hunted Siegmund in *Die Walküre* (*The Valkyrie*). More notably, Ada's scene and aria, in which she dreads the torment she will cause her husband, is the first of Wagner's vocal pieces to denote mental affliction. The vast finales, especially the septet that closes act 2, show his skill at manipulating large-scale forces. But however agreeable and, at isolated moments, dramatically apt the music, it is rarely under the composer's control. For example, at the point where Wagner should be able to summon up his most poignant melody, when Arindal sings his wife back to life, he produces a tune of striking banality, even though some minutes earlier, at a less important moment, he has given the same character a passage of haunting beauty.

Perhaps *The Fairies* is of most interest as a draft for the later works. One can hear in embryo the generous melodies of *Tannhäuser* and *Lohengrin*, while later dramatic themes are also foreshadowed, in particular the suggestion that pure love requires blind trust and the concern with redemption by love upon which the whole of the *Ring*-cycle rests. Above all, the conclusion, in which Ada and Arindal renounce the physical world for the erotic delights of fairyland, prefigures later works in which the tangible world is likewise renounced.

On his return to Leipzig in January 1834, Wagner submitted *The Fairies* to the Court Theatre and, although the authorities had some problems with the style, for a time it looked as if the opera might be performed. Wagner himself, however, vigorously resisted the theatre's production practices. Using stock scenery and costumes from other fairy-plays and operas, the Leipzig production was to have had an Oriental setting, even though Wagner had drawn his characters largely from Ossianic (Gaelic) mythology. Such disregard for the author's or composer's intentions was entirely normal in the theatre of the time, but Wagner was so uncompromising in his insistence that his work be represented on stage in a manner compatible with his own conception that the Leipzig authorities eventually withdrew the opera from consideration. Wagner, who was moving on to new projects, quickly lost interest in it, but perhaps it occurred to him even then that in order to realize his operas as he wished, he might have to run his own theatre.

The next major event in his career was his appointment in July 1834 to the musical directorship of the Bethmann Theatrical Company, which was centered in Magdeburg but toured small towns in the Thüringer Wald during the summer. At his first interview with Heinrich Bethmann in Lauchstädt, Wagner was so repelled by the moral squalor of the theatre and the impossible performing conditions—he was expected to conduct

Don Giovanni on two days' notice, without an orchestral rehearsal—that he was on the point of refusing the offer. At the door of the house where he was lodging for the night, however, he met the actress Minna Planer. At this point, artistic and moral scruples were thrown to the winds, and Wagner accepted the appointment.

By the time he had arrived in Lauchstadt, Wagner was not sexually innocent. He had conceived an infatuation for a Bohemian count's daughter that had lasted on and off for a couple of years, but his first real affair probably took place in Würzburg. This led him to believe, not without good cause, that, despite his relatively small body and oversized head, he was unusually attractive to women. Minna, who was stunningly beautiful as a young woman, may have struck him initially as little more than a highly desirable conquest. Letters he wrote at the time hint at other affairs and even suggest that he was willing to share Minna with his best friend, Theodor Apel.[7] It was not until several months after the theatre company had settled in Magdeburg for the winter that they were publicly accepted as lovers. The association was a liberating experience for neither of them. Minna was more concerned with financial security than with the quality of her sexual life and was uncertain whether to become too closely involved, while Wagner became increasingly dependent on her emotionally. In November 1835, when she left Magdeburg to pursue a lucrative offer from the Königsstadt Theatre in Berlin, she was persuaded to return only by the most abject letters from her lover. Not without cause did Wagner in later years describe his appointment to the Bethmann company as marking the time when care entered his life (*ML*, 1, 116).

His career as musical director of the Company was successful, and, despite the reduced salary he was forced to accept due to Bethmann's chronically impending bankruptcy, he did not complain in his autobiography of artistic demoralization. Although the quality of orchestral playing and vocal ensemble was far below that of Dresden and Leipzig, there was probably sufficient musical and dramatic expertise to satisfy him, especially since the appointment gave him his first extended experience as a conductor. Moreover, Bethmann, who had complacently tolerated his first wife's status as a royal favorite, had direct access to the Saxon treasury. As a result, when his company was on the verge of breaking up in the summer of 1835, he was saved by a royal subsidy. Wagner, at his own request and expense, then traveled through Germany to hire singers for the newly constituted company. His efforts did little to improve matters financially, and, by the following spring, the company had broken up permanently. Its last performance was the première of Wagner's next opera, *Das Liebesverbot* (*The Ban on Love*).

The striking contrast between Wagner's first and second operas reflects the notably systematic approach to composition characteristic of his early career as an opera composer. Despite his impulsive habits of study, he set out to master in turn each of the major national styles that comprised the repertoire of contemporary opera houses. *The Fairies* had demonstrated his facility in the German Romantic vein. After this, as he indicated in a letter to Apel, he planned to travel to Italy to "write an Italian opera, & depending on what happens, perhaps more. Then, when we are brown and strong, we will turn to France. In Paris I shall write a French opera, and God knows, where I will be then" (*SB*, 1, 167–168). Although his travels did not occur as described in this letter, it foretold accurately enough his future artistic productivity.

The Ban on Love is Wagner's only work that is largely in the Italian style that was universally popular in Europe during the 1830s and 1840s. Before embarking on its composition, he published two essays, "On German Opera" and "Pasticcio," in which he attacked German opera composers for being too pedantic, concerned with detail and with writing lyrical rather than dramatic music, a criticism not without application to *The Fairies*. He instead championed Italian opera composers who placed greater dependency on melody, thereby conveying the action in "a single bold and emphatic stroke" (*GSB*, VII, 9). Boldness is without doubt the salient quality of *The Ban on Love*.

This work is unique as the only extant operatic adaptation of *Measure for Measure*.[8] This is probably because the dark irony of Shakespeare's action and the low comedy of the Viennese brothels is not well suited to musical representation. Wagner's adaptation, however, avoids the irony. Instead, under the influence of Laube and the Young Germans and as an expression of the awakening he experienced through his affair with Minna, Wagner intended this opera as a glorification of total sexual freedom. He shifted the action from Vienna to Palermo, from a city where the realities of the body were confronted to a symbolic realm of harmless carnival, cut the figure of the Duke (who became instead an absent king), and renamed Angelo as Friedrich, a baleful German viceroy concerned solely with banning carnival and free love.

The opera opens with a rowdy scene in which the brothels are being cleared out, but with the unrefined realism of the original somewhat modified. Wagner has concentrated Shakespeare's gallery of grotesques into the single, generic *commedia dell' arte* figure of Brighella. Lucio, no longer a venal rake, becomes a good-hearted *bon vivant*; far from indulging in boundless sensuality, he conceives a notably single-minded passion for Isabella. Since the low life is more contained than in Shakespeare, the plot is less complex. With the Duke excised, Isabella, faced with Friedrich's demand that she sleep with him, has to arrange the bed trick herself and serve as the chief intriguer.

These changes mean that *The Ban on Love*, far from being an irregularly plotted Shakespearean play, is closer in spirit to the well-made play, a form pioneered by the French dramatist Eugène Scribe (1791–1861), in which dramatic action is contained within a tightly structured plot that demonstrates the logical workings of cause and effect. The rational perspective on human conduct implicit in this form made the well-made play the preeminent genre of the popular spoken theatre in Europe in the middle decades of the nineteenth century. Wagner's tailoring of Shakespeare's play to the restricted dimensions of the form underscores his desire to achieve a success in terms of the conventional theatre, but it is the cause of the opera's main dramaturgical failing.[9] This is apparent above all in Wagner's inability to make Isabella a credible character who can serve multiple functions. As the pivotal figure in the action, she starts as a pious novice who indignantly rejects Lucio's advances, but the moment she tangles with Friedrich, her character loses all consistency. Not only does she discover previously unsuspected depths of feeling in reaction to his proposal, but she also hits upon the idea of the bed trick herself. She creates the plot that will catch Friedrich, turns into a popular leader who assures the mob that she will stand for the rights of carnival and, finally, discovering sexual desire, throws herself with abandon into Lucio's arms. Because Wagner was not yet skilled in depicting progressive contradictions in character, there is no sense of growth in Isabella's personality, and she remains a collection of contrary traits rather than a coherent character. Only Friedrich, in the opera's one major aria, achieves complexity as he determines both to possess Isabella and to fall victim to the law. Here the opera moves from a concern with the mechanics of plot to the richer plane of intricate conflict within character, in which the experience of sexual desire obliterates all other considerations, even that of survival itself. But with his tightly constructed plot, which concludes with a series of disguises and unmaskings reminiscent of W. A. Mozart's *Marriage of Figaro*, Wagner gave himself no opportunity to investigate these potentially tragic dimensions. The cheerful conclusion, in which the crowd surges out to welcome the returning King once the lovers are united, suggests that, in contrast to Shakespeare, Wagner believed human beings to be eminently governable creatures.

Musically, *The Ban on Love* has earned little respect. Later in life, Wagner described it as "horrible . . . execrable . . . disgusting."[10] It has subsequently been dismissed by a leading musicologist as "a piece of impertinence and shameless imitation."[11] These judgments are unjust. Whatever its shortcomings as drama, the opera in fact demonstrates the diversity of the young Wagner's talents. Daniel Auber's *La muette de Portici* (*The Mute Girl of Portici*, 1828), one of the most widely performed French grand operas, is commonly held to have been his main inspiration, but modern listeners may be more taken by the passages in which Wagner borrowed from his Italian contemporaries, whose *bel canto* operas were written specifically to display the beauty and virtuosity of performers' voices. Skillfully incorporated into the score are sequences of the florid cantiliena that was so attractive a feature of the operas of Vincenzo Bellini (1801–1835). Similarly, in the scenes involving Brighella, one finds intricate and rhythmically complex duets that might be attributed to Gioacchino Rossini (1792–1868), whose comic operas (*opera buffa*) enjoyed universal popularity in the 1830s. Even the urgent romantic melodies of the early works of Giuseppe Verdi (1831–1901) are uncannily prefigured in an arietta given to Claudio at the start of act 2.

The eclecticism of the music might be compared to Shakespeare's alternations between low comedy and pathos, but Wagner's contrasts are haphazard. Like some of the Italian composers he imitated, not all Wagner's melodies are specific, and few express accurately the emotions they are designed to represent. As a result, the music too frequently lacks authenticity as dramatic language, so that ultimately *The Ban on Love*, like *The Fairies*, is of primary interest for moments that prefigure the later Wagner. The most famous of these is the "Dresden Amen," which appears in *Lohengrin* and *Parsifal*, but here used to establish the pious atmosphere of the nunnery. Whole melodies that would eventually appear in *The Flying Dutchman*, *Tannhäuser*, and *Lohengrin* turn up first in *The Ban on Love*, often to the confusion of the modern listener, since they occur in situations radically different from those in the more familiar later operas.

The fiasco of the opening nights of *The Ban on Love* is a classic among opera tales, told with great liveliness by Wagner in his autobiography. Due to a backstage quarrel between the husband of the soprano singing Isabella and the tenor playing Claudio, who was the soprano's lover, the second performance had to be canceled. This was not especially disastrous, since there were only three people in the audience. One of these was Wagner's landlady, whose main preoccupation was whether he could pay his rent. Wagner left town soon after, deeply in debt and questioning his vocation.

This questioning became more urgent during his subsequent stay in Berlin. Minna had taken an engagement in Königsberg, while Wagner remained in Berlin hoping to have *The Ban on Love* performed at the Königsstadt Theatre. His failure in this project only revived and intensified his disillusionment with the theatre, since theatre was now causing him personal as well as professional anguish. From childhood on, theatre in various guises had nurtured his imaginative life, but now, infatuated with Minna, he felt it as a hostile force that was subverting the integrity of his emotions. In an agonized letter, he wrote to her how he had heard her reputation slandered by a traveler in a restaurant. He attributed this to the automatic disrepute women suffered the moment they became actresses. In a passage worthy of the most rabid antitheatricalist, he longed to take her away from the stage:

> A girl or woman of the theatre is really too much on display, & I consider it to be my most sacred duty, tc do everything to take you away from the theatre as soon as possible. Under no circumstances may you come to Berlin as an actress,—it would be much better if I had my good little wife all to myself & not for every idle gaper in the theatre. You will be much more sacred then! (*SB*, I, 291)

But with no work available in Berlin, he had to travel to Minna, not she to him. On 7 July 1836, he left Berlin to join her in Königsberg, where he was given the post of assistant musical director, with a promise of the full directorship the following April.

Soon after his arrival, Minna and Richard committed what was possibly the most foolhardy action of their lives—they married. This they did with full knowledge of how incompatible they were, for they even quarreled in the corridor outside the pastor's room as they were waiting to arrange the wedding. Their incompatibility was nowhere more apparent than in their differing attitudes toward theatre. While Wagner had yet to develop his vision of the ideal theatre, he was already becoming aware of the gap between theatre in actuality and the potential that he felt certain it could achieve. Minna had no understanding of this. For her, the theatre was nothing more than a place to earn a living, and, like most other actresses of the time, including all three of Wagner's sisters, she was only too pleased to leave it when she found financial security. While Minna would never understand her husband's artistic ambitions, he, falling ever more deeply into debt, was the last man to offer her the security she needed.

Things came to a head the following year, in May 1837, when Minna left Königsberg in the company of a businessman. Wagner set out in pursuit but, lacking sufficient funds, was unable to travel far. When eventually he ran her to ground, she was with her family in Dresden. After a summer spent in inconclusive negotiations, Wagner traveled alone to Riga, Latvia, where he had been appointed musical director of the German theatre. In October, the errant wife eventually rejoined her chastened husband, and the two set up house on a more permanent basis. As Minna had now retired from the stage, the potential for friction between the two was reduced.

Despite this marginal increase in personal happiness, the eighteen months they spent in Riga were far from happy. Wagner's dislike of the realities of the theatrical life grew so intense that eventually he fulfilled only the minimum duties required of him. This was as much the fault of the theatre director, Karl von Holtei, as it was of Wagner himself. Holtei's tastes, which complemented those of the majority of the audience, ran more toward light opera and fashionable French and Italian works against which Wagner, given the failure of *The Ban on Love*, was beginning to develop a violent antipathy. In particular, Wagner concluded that theatre defeated the cause of good music and that success in one field automatically meant failure in the other. Since he also found members of the Riga ensemble to be vain, impudent, uneducated, undisciplined, and promiscuous, he was drawn more to the practice of pure music. In fact, the most satisfying of his public duties in Riga was the introduction of concerts of orchestral music into the city's cultural life.

Wagner's ambition to unite music and the drama was not, however, dead. In the summer of 1837, he had read Edward George Earle Bulwer-Lytton's novel *Rienzi, the Last of the Roman Tribunes* and, recalling a suggestion from his friend Apel, set to work on a libretto based on it. He wrote the score for the first two acts in Riga but did not complete the last three until October 1840, when he was living in Paris. Nevertheless, since in writing *Rienzi* he was completing his process of apprenticeship (as outlined in the letter to Apel from Magdeburg), this opera should most properly be considered as a work predating his artistic maturity.

Rienzi has always been an embarrassment to Wagnerians. Even after he had achieved worldwide fame with work of a very different nature, it remained among the most frequently performed of his works, and, because he was constantly in need of money, he relied upon revenues from it, even though he had renounced the principles upon which it was composed. It is the one stage work that Wagner seems not to have written from an inner need; instead, he deliberately modeled it upon a genre for which he later claimed to have little respect—the grand operas of Gasparo Spontini (1774–1851) and Giacomo Meyerbeer (1791–1864).

Wagner's relationship with Meyerbeer has always been one of the more questionable and distasteful aspects of his controversial life. Even as a young man in Würzburg, Wagner had complained about the artistic inadequacies of *Robert the Devil*, the first opera, composed to a text by

Scribe, that brought Meyerbeer international fame. Later in life, Wagner inveighed against what he considered Meyerbeer's tendency to indulge in grandiose, historical spectacle and in massive musical numbers for purely momentary effect with no dramatic integrity. Nevertheless, this overt theatricality, which was fully exercised in Meyerbeer's most celebrated opera, *Les Huguenots* (1836), also to a text by Scribe, made him the most acclaimed and wealthiest opera composer of the day. Artistically, Wagner exploited this reputation in the composition of *Rienzi* and personally benefited from Meyerbeer's generous patronage, for the older composer did much to help the younger get his start. Wagner, however, would later vilify Meyerbeer—for artistic insincerity, for supposedly undermining Wagner's interests, and, notoriously, for being a Jew. Meyerbeer was the first and perhaps the most celebrated victim of Wagner's anti-Semitism.

In his youth, however, both Wagner's understanding of artistic integrity and his anti-Semitism were far from being fully developed, a condition to which *Rienzi* is testimony. Set in fourteenth-century Rome, the opera dramatizes the defeat of the turbulent patricians by the plebeian tribune *Rienzi*, his elevation to the leadership of Rome, and his subsequent fall, due to his pride, the machinations of politicians, and the fickleness of the mob. Dramatically, the opera has all the features of nineteenth-century melodrama. Characters essentially embody the ideas they represent; ciphers of the action and its moral structure, rarely do they show evidence of a volition that might challenge that function. This artistic approach causes considerable confusion, above all in understanding the main character and his fate. At the start, Rienzi is a charismatic figure of whom all are in awe, but, by act 2, there are signs in the stage directions describing his fantastic costume that this power is going to his head. Nevertheless, Rienzi never becomes a Coriolanus, the victim of his own pride, even though one senses that Wagner wishes to represent him as such. Instead, he is destroyed by his habit of naïvely forgiving his enemies in situations where ruthlessness is required and by the unaccountable (because dramatically unanticipated) jealousy of his associates. Furthermore, at the height of his supposed "corruption" as a leader, he sings the solemn "Prayer," the most imposing aria in the opera, which impresses him on the audience's memory as a divinely appointed leader. The lack of irony, which is a consequence of such characterization, suggests that the opera can credibly be interpreted as an idealization of dictatorship. There is likewise a totalitarian dimension in the political ideals embodied in the action. As has been pointed out, the patricians are condemned not for the social privileges they assume but for their libertine life.[12] In fact, the idea of an aristocracy wedded to plebeian stock is presented as an ideal to be emulated. The oppressiveness of this vision is mitigated in part by the utopian vision of peace, but, in general, both the staging and music emphasize the idealization of force.

Rienzi is characteristic of its creator in its excessiveness. Lasting well over four hours (the première in Dresden ran for six), the opera is a seemingly neverending series of processions, battles, and triumphal scenes. Although the stage direction that "all citizens of Rome capable of bearing arms march off ready for battle and in order" is not perhaps to be taken literally, it is a good indication of the gigantic dimensions of the opera. At times, the stage directions are effective, but their impact is usually lost in a seemingly indiscriminate exploitation of all the known stage effects of grand opera. As for the music, it is difficult not to agree with Ernest Newman, who found fewer memorable passages in *Rienzi* than in Wagner's other stage works.[13] One immense ensemble is piled upon another. The whole is wearisomely noisy, with finales extended to the point of absurdity. Monotonous march rhythms abound, even in ensembles where they have little place, and, like the characters themselves, the music is persistently rhetorical. Only on a few occasions, such as in the orchestral introduction to act 3 or the chorus of women during the battle that follows, does the music capture a specific emotion, here the fear of war and its monstrous destruction. Most of the time, the music seems intended to incite to battle and hence is rhetorical rather than descriptive. In general, *Rienzi* is Wagner's least attractive work.

In the middle of composing the opera, Wagner reached a crisis in his affairs with the Riga theatre. Steadily intensifying strains between him and Holtei led to the latter's resignation, but not before the manager had made certain that Wagner would lose the musical directorship. Once again unemployed and ever deeper in debt, Wagner and his wife were forced to flee secretly across the Russo-Prussian border in order to escape his creditors. After some adventures, including an accident in a cart that may have injured Minna so badly that she could not have children, the fugitive couple set sail from the tiny port of Pillau on a journey that would end in Paris. That journey also ended the days of Wagner's apprenticeship.

NOTES

1. Quoted in Curt von Westernhagen, *Wagner: A Biography*, 2 vols. (Cambridge: Cambridge University Press, 1978), 1: 5.

2. Richard Wagner, *Mein Leben*, 2d ed. (Munich: Bruckmann, 1915), 6 (henceforward *ML*). All translations from the German are my own, unless otherwise indicated.

3. Eduard Devrient, *Geschichte der deutschen Schauspielkunst*, ed. Rolf Kabel and Christoph Trilse, 2 vols. (Munich: Langen Müller, 1967), II: 208.

4. Richard Wagner, *Gesammelte Schriften und Briefe*, ed. Julius Knapp, 14 vols. (Leipzig: Hesse & Becker, n.d. [1914]), I: 39–40 (henceforward *GSB*).

5. Mary Burrell, *Richard Wagner: His Life and Works from 1813 to 1834* (London, 1898), 90.

6. John Deathridge and Carl Dahlhaus, *The New Grove Wagner* (New York: Norton, 1984), 7.

7. Richard Wagner, *Sämtliche Briefe*, ed. Gertrud Strobel and Werner Wolf, 8 vols. (Leipzig: Deutscher Verlag fur Müsik, 1967), I: 164 (henceforward *SB*).

8. Winton Dean, "Shakespeare in the Opera House," *Shakespeare Survey* 18 (1965): 88–93.

9. See Simon Williams, "Wagner's *Das Liebesverbot*: From Shakespeare to the Well-Made play," *The Opera Quarterly* 3: 4 (Winter 1985–86): 56–69.

10. Cosima Wagner, *Diaries*, trans. Geoffrey Skeleton, 2 vols. (New York and London: Harcourt, 1977, 1980), 2: 300 (henceforward *CWD*).

11. Robert Gutman, *Richard Wagner: The Man, His Mind, and His Music* (New York: Harcourt, 1968), 95.

12. Theodore Adorno, *In Search of Wagner*, trans. Rodney Livingstone (London: NLB, 1981), 13.

13. Ernest Newman, *Wagner as Man and Artist* (New York: Knopf, 1924), 261–2.

Chapter 2

Bohemian in Paris

Wagner's journey to Paris was probably the most frightening experience of his life.The voyage, via London, should, at the height of the summer, have taken a week at most, but the boat encountered a series of storms that put it at the mercy of the elements for over three weeks. The event that stuck most firmly in Wagner's memory was the moment the ship found a brief respite from the storm in the peaceful Norwegian harbor of Sandvika. In the middle of August, the Wagners reached London. There they stayed for a week, trying without success to contact Bulwer-Lytton, the author of *Rienzi*. Since the London musical world was dormant in summer, they traveled on to Boulogne in France where Meyerbeer was staying.

Wagner was not entirely unknown to Meyerbeer, because he had written to him in 1837, soliciting his patronage for *The Ban on Love*. Meyerbeer received him in Boulogne, listened to him read the first three acts of *Rienzi*, and examined the full orchestral score of the first two acts. He gave the younger man a letter of introduction to Charles Edmund Duponchel, the director of the Paris Opéra, so, when Wagner arrived in Paris in the middle of September, he hoped that he would quickly overcome the barriers of privilege and commercial interest that stood between him and a successful career in the Parisian theatre.

He was to be brutally disappointed. Meyerbeer's letter had no effect. Duponchel had no interest in an unknown German composer, nor did the rest of the theatrical and musical world of Paris. Through the good services of Meyerbeer, *The Ban on Love* was accepted by the Théâtre de la Renaissance in the spring of 1840, but the theatre went bankrupt before the work could be performed. Later, Wagner managed to have extracts auditioned at the Opéra before the composer Edouard Monnais and the playwright Eugene Scribe, but they showed polite interest and nothing more. Such rejection was typical of the miserable two-and-a-half years he spent in Paris. Incapable of gaining entrance into the most prestigious network of urban theatres in Europe, Wagner was forced to earn his living copying music and writing the occasional journalistic piece for periodicals in Paris and Dresden, which brought him nothing but the barest minimum needed for subsistence. He depended mainly on these payments and on sporadic handouts from friends and family members, particularly his sister Cäcilie, then living in Paris, the wife of Eduard Avenarius, an agent for Brockhaus, the Leipzig publishers. Even then, his means were so straitened that he may have spent some days in debtors' prison in November 1840.

Professional failure was mitigated somewhat by happiness in his personal life. Minna's devotion to Wagner intensified, bringing a temporary joy to their otherwise bleak marriage. In addition, Wagner, who later in life lost many friends by exploiting them without scruple, formed the warmest and freest companionships he would ever know with three German exiles—Gottfried Anders, an impoverished librarian, Samuel Lehrs, a diligent but obscure scholar, and Ernst Benedikt Kietz, an incorrigible pederast and talented portraitist who could never complete a commission but who made one of the first portraits we have of Wagner (Illustration 1). In letters written after he had left Paris, it is clear that these friendships allowed Wagner to feel some nostalgia for the city that had treated him with such indifference. Rarely in the future would he so generously acknowledge the benign influence of those close to him.

While the years in Paris did nothing to advance his public career, they were vital for his growth as an artist. The precise nature of this growth can best be gathered from the essays and short stories that he published during this period. These writings from Paris are unique in his substantial literary output, for, while much of the later prose is virtually unreadable for its prolixity and weighty verbiage, the Parisian essays are models of simplicity. They demonstrate too a critical acumen keen enough to suggest that had Wagner cultivated his literary ability exclusively, he might have become one of the century's more significant critics. The few short stories from this time demonstrate the influence of E.T.A. Hoffmann, a writer who had meant much to him during his adolescence and early manhood.

These writings reveal Wagner's growing mistrust of Paris as the center of a burgeoning civilization devoted primarily to amassing as much wealth as possible. It was, of course, this affluence and the power that went with it that had attracted Wagner to Paris in the first place, but, excluded from

Illustration 1. Richard Wagner during the Paris years. (Drawing by Ernst Benedikt Kietz. Reproduced by permission of the Nationalarchiv der Richard-Wagner-Stiftung/Richard-Wagner-Gedenkstätte, Bayreuth.)

it, he grew to hate it. France accordingly came to represent in his imagination an ostentatious society that worshiped the superficial, and valued people purely for their wealth. In contrast, he came to see Germany as a land where "inwardness" was prized, where people turned from social life to find inspiration within themselves. Such generalities about France and Germany were more commonplace than Wagner probably liked to think, for they had been the stock-in-trade of Germans' writings on the difference between their own and French national culture since the middle of the eighteenth century. In Wagner's case, however, these ideas were given renewed vitality, first by his personal experiences and secondly by their specific application to music and theatre.

For Wagner, the icon of French art was the virtuoso. In their concern to display their technique, virtuosi, whether singers, instrumental soloists, or conductors, "provide no warmth but they glitter" (*GSB*, VII, 67). *How* singers sang, Wagner complained, was more important than *what* they sang. Consequently, the music became twisted, often beyond all recognition, to accommodate the demands of the exhibitionistic performer. He described a performance of *Don Giovanni*, which, despite its illustrious cast, was unusually restrained until Rubini, the Don Ottavio of the evening, delivered his "famous trill from A to B" (*GSB*, VII, 74), causing an uproar in the audience. Mozart's opera, Wagner suggested, was "only a wooden puppet clothed in the drapery of pure virtuosity as a formal justification for the existence of the work of music" (*GSB*, VII, 76). Wagner objected as well to the insensitive staging that operas frequently received. Not surprisingly, the première of *Der Freischütz* at the Paris Opéra drew from him sustained critical fire. The original spoken dialogue, fundamental to the atmosphere of the work, was replaced by recitative by Hector Berlioz; the acting was slick and melodramatic, while the production itself was entirely inconsistent, with the Prince's court being dressed in Turkish costume amidst peasants in Bohemian costume. In the Opéra's defense, few in the audience would have noted the incongruity, as such habits were a holdover from the days of *opera seria*, the portentous tragic operas of the eighteenth century that were set in the most exotic locales with no concern in either costumes or setting for historical or geographical accuracy.

Wagner was not blindly critical of the Parisian theatre. Recalling these years, he acnowledged that the production of Meyerbeer's *Les Huguenots* made him aware of the impact that could be made by "extremely careful and effective production" (*ML*, I, 266)—a comment indicating that the habits of *opera seria* production were dying. Wagner was always prepared to grant French playwrights and composers great facility at devising and representing effective dramatic situations, but, since these were executed in the service of an institution as ostentatious as the Parisian theatre, the very capacity to be effectively theatrical was itself to be distrusted. One suspects that Wagner's growing dislike of theatre was a virtue culled from necessity. Due to the high price of tickets at the Opéra, he visited that institution only four times in two years. He found the cheaper Opéra Comique to be repellent, for its productions were marked by a "complete absence of common theatrical warmth." As for the spoken theatre, he appears to have grown utterly indifferent to it; on being offered free tickets to see the famous actress Rachel at the Comédie Française, he turned them down (*ML*, I, 267–268).

This reaction against the commodification of performance in the Parisian theatres represents the first phase in Wagner's ever-shifting theories as to the nature of art and of music theatre in particular. The very wealth of Paris, he contended, nullified its capacity to nurture art, for there the successful artist was forced constantly to write or compose with an eye to the effect the material would have upon the audience. This need inevitably involved a compromise between the artist's personal vision, which should be paramount, and the desire of audiences, who wished solely to be entertained. In reaction, Wagner started to conceive of the artist as a superior being who dealt with the world at his peril: "Every experience lets [the genius] feel that he is in an inferior sphere, and that things will really turn out well for him only when he himself takes up an inferior guise" (*GSB*, VII, 139–40). Instead, Wagner insisted that the artist should "communicate his inner bliss to human hearts" (*GSB*, VII, 141) by ignoring everything that compromised his vision. Artists, he felt, are a breed apart, persons who should not be subject to the mundane transactions of social life and should deal with the world only on their own terms. With Paris standing in the German exile's mind as the apogee of modern materialism, his homeland appeared increasingly to be a haven where the "true artist" was nurtured.

Such opposing concepts of France and Germany were far from exclusive to this rejected and homesick young artist. The German essayist and poet Heinrich Heine, who had lived in Paris in voluntary exile since 1831 and whom Wagner met during this period, had published a series of essays on the Parisian theatre. In these, he argued that while French comedy was "pretty and funny," it was inhumane in spirit, without any concern for humanity or for the casualties of social progress. This cold indifference Heine ascribed to the widespread breakdown of marriages caused by the onset of industrialization in post-Napoleonic society. In contrast, the more stable German society was sustained by an inviolate traditional family structure. Theatre more appropriately belonged to a publicly oriented society, such as France, than to the more private Germany. While the essence of French tragedy lay in arousing in a public audience passions more extreme than those encountered in everyday life, in Germany the heart of tragedy lay in its poetry rather than its action; this "works more effectively on the lonely reader than on a great gathering."[1] In his discussion of music in the theatre, which was marked by a distinct appreciation for the spectacle of French grand opera, Heine acknowledged that Meyerbeer's work was in essence "more social than individual." For Meyerbeer, the "model of urbanity" offered by France was more congenial than the private, poetic, and essentially untheatrical culture of Germany.

Wagner's commitment to his beliefs, strengthened no doubt by conversations with Heine and other German exiles, was also augmented by a growing confidence in his creative powers. He completed *Rienzi* in November 1840. Given his ideas about the nature of the true artist, the final stages of composition must have been trying, for this opera, composed in the grand style of Meyerbeer, was clearly designed to please its audiences and written to make a public reputation, rather than to express the "inner bliss" of its creator. Long before he had finished *Rienzi*, the idea for his next opera was already germinating in his imagination. In the spring of 1841, he managed to scrape together sufficient funds to move to the village of Meudon outside Paris, where he stayed until the autumn. Here he wrote what was to be his first major contribution to the operatic repertoire and the first work that bore the unmistakable stamp of his own genius—*Der fliegende Holländer* (*The Flying Dutchman*).

By the mid-nineteenth century, the legend of the Flying Dutchman had become a common literary and dramatic property. Wagner may first have decided on the subject in Riga where he read a satirical treatment of it in Heine's *Memoiren des Herrn von Schnabelwopski* (*Memoirs of Herr von Schnabelwopski*). The stormy voyage to Paris gave the legend a powerful personal meaning, especially since Wagner thought that the sailors blamed him personally for the appalling weather. In fact, he used the cries that they uttered as they found haven in Sandvika for the calls of the Norwegian sailors that open the action. But even this, the first of Wagner's more personal works, was initially conceived for the Paris Opéra as a one-act curtain-raiser to an evening of ballet. He submitted the prose scenario, completed in May 1841, to the Opéra, which for once was interested but only if a librettist and composer of its choice set the story. Wagner sold them the scenario for 500 francs, and about eighteen months later, *Le Vaisseau fantôme*, with music by Pierre-Louis Dietsch, was unsuccessfully staged at the Opéra. Ironically, it was the sale of the scenario that enabled Wagner to move to Meudon where he found the peace to compose his own version.

Wagner incorporated into this version most of the features first included by Heine in his prose narrative, though without Heine's satirical purpose. Because a Dutch sailor once rashly swore a vow, the Devil has condemned him to sail the oceans for eternity. He can be saved only if he finds a woman prepared to sacrifice her life for him, and he is allowed to land once every seven years to search for her. Wagner's Dutchman comes ashore at Sandvika; there he meets the merchant Daland who, in return for the Dutchman's riches, promises him his daughter Senta's hand. Senta is already obsessed by a portrait of the Dutchman that hangs in her house, and, when he arrives in person to woo her, she has no difficulty in recognizing him, binding herself to him for life. However, she also has a suitor, the hunter Erik. Due to a series of circumstances that he misunderstands, the Dutchman thinks Senta has been unfaithful to him with Erik, so he sets sail once again. Senta ensures his salvation by throwing herself from a cliff.

The Flying Dutchman is pivotal in Wagner's output as the first work in which the salient features of the dramas of his maturity are apparent. Both the stage and music are used consistently to articulate the action, in direct opposition to his perception of grand opera as staged in Paris, where he argued that the stage was used merely for spectacle and display. In an essay written some years after composing the opera, he gave instructions as to how it should be performed. He began by insisting on an

> exact correspondence between what happens on stage and what happens in the orchestra. . . . In particular, the ships and the sea require the extraordinary attention of the stage director. . . . The first scene of the opera has to generate that frame of mind that makes it possible for the spectator to understand for himself the wonderful appearance of the "Flying Dutchman"; it must therefore be handled with exceptional love. (*GSB*, IX, 44–45)

In other words, the prime purpose of both the music and staging must be to lead the audience into a sympathetic acceptance of the Dutchman's predicament. From the "French" concern with the glamorous externals of a dramatic action, Wagner turned to the "German" preoccupation with inwardness, with the sufferings of the dynamic mind. Thus, while one of the more notable aspects of the opera's music is its graphic representation of stormy weather and tempestuous seas, the purely mimetic quality is incidental, its sole function being to draw the audience into the troubled psyche of the Dutchman.

This redirection of dramatic focus leads to several important innovative features. First, the action is unusually simple. The complex intrigue that characterized the grand opera of his day would not have served Wagner's purpose, since it would deflect attention from the single concern of the Dutchman's mental condition. Indeed, when conventional plot elements do intrude, such as the moment when the Dutchman thinks Senta is unfaithful because he misunderstands an overheard conversation between her and Erik, they seem false to the purpose of the opera. A simpler and more effective motivation for his departure might have been devised. Nevertheless, the comparatively unembellished plot was novel, which led a perceptive contemporary to label it a "dramatic ballad," rather than a "romantic opera," as Wagner himself did.[2] Wagner, who feared that some "inchoate" aspects might lead modern playwrights to denounce his "poem as a piece of impudence that deserves to be punished" (*GSB*, I, 95), nevertheless claimed that with *The Flying Dutchman* he had ceased being a "manufacturer of texts."

The central character is markedly different from the conventional operatic hero. Drawn from neither historical sources nor romantic fairy-tales, Wagner considered him a mythic figure drawn from the imagination of the people. As such, he embodies an ahistorical primal trait, identified as "the longing after rest from amid the storms of life." The Dutchman himself is a

> curious mixture of the character of the Wandering Jew with that of Odysseus. . . . Like Ahasveros, he longs for his sufferings to be ended by death; the Dutchman can win this salvation, denied to the Wandering Jew, through a woman, who sacrifices herself out of love for him. (*GSB*, I, 94)

In Wagnerian prose, such sentiments sound inflated, but, expressed through music, they gain credibility, for the audience senses directly the pain of the Dutchman's sufferings. The solo he sings as he first comes on shore, "Die Frist ist um" ("The time is up"), is not intended to display the range and flexibility of the voice, which was the normal function of an entrance aria for a principal character in the popular *opera seria* of Rossini; likewise, it is not designed to project an ideal image of heroic action, which was characteristic of grand opera. Rather, exploiting the already established themes of storm and fury, the Dutchman sings of eternal restlessness and the denial of oblivion. Toward the end of this solo, he grows into an apocalyptic figure, whose sufferings, announced by trumpet calls from the orchestra, associate him with the Day of Judgment itself.

The predominantly subjective vision that Wagner encourages us to take of the Dutchman leads to stylistic inconsistency. It is not difficult to fit Senta into the action. From the moment she is seen gazing at the Dutchman's portrait to the accompaniment of musical themes associated with him, it is clear that she lives in his mental realm. In their one encounter, the great duet that comprises the second half of act 2, the Dutchman and Senta begin singing distinct but complementary melodies, which rise to a climax of ecstatic union as she declares her fidelity to him until death. Other characters are less easily incorporated, for they move in a more literally physical sphere than the Dutchman and Senta. For example, Daland, Senta's materialistic father, is given reassuringly pleasant, even bland, music, reminiscent at times of *opera buffa*, the Italian comic opera that still enjoyed an immense vogue in European opera houses. This music contrasts strikingly with the gloomier tones of the Dutchman and at times is clearly inappropriate. At the end of act 1, for example, in a duet in which the two men agree to Senta's marriage, the Dutchman's pain is entirely absorbed by Daland's cozy melody. If Daland is a remnant of an earlier theatrical tradition, which was becoming increasingly alien to Wagner, so too is Erik, though more effectively so. When Erik first enters in act 2, the orchestra and his vocal line both suggest that he is a conventional romantic hero from contemporary Italian opera; nevertheless, his duet with Senta has neither the symmetry nor the extended melodic passages familiar from Italian opera. Broken phrases express his panic at the loss of her affection and his growing uneasiness at her fixation with the portrait of the Dutchman. Pure musical form has been sacrificed to explore the disintegration of Eric's love and Senta's sanity.

Most crucially perhaps, *The Flying Dutchman* represents a major advance in Wagner's quest for a new musical dramatic language. Some years after completing the opera, he wrote to a friend explaining that he felt he could maintain the listener's attention only by

> holding him spellbound in such a strange state of mind so that even those with little appreciation of poetry can be persuaded to be at ease with this gloomiest of legends. So I made sure that my music was of the same nature: to achieve this goal I was able to look neither to the left nor right, making not the slightest concession to modern taste. . . . From the very start I had to give up the modern arrangement into arias, duets, finales, etc., and instead tell the story in one breath, as a good poem should be told. (*SB*, II, 314–315.)

Here Wagner identified what was to be among his most important contributions to the development of opera as a dramatic medium. What he referred to as the "modern arrangement" of operas by musical "numbers" had been universally practiced by librettists and composers, and his own earlier operas had been constructed mainly according to the numbers' principle. Nonetheless, he now considered that dividing the music into discrete numbers disrupted the flow of the dramatic action. In the place of numbers, he wished to compose unbroken music that allowed the story of the opera to be told "in a single breath," with the sole aim of articulating the action. In truth, his demand for continuity of dramatic music was not quite as original as he claimed. Rossini, especially in his *opera seria* of the 1820s, had begun to introduce more extended passages of music in which the drama was sustained unbroken for passages lasting fifteen minutes or longer. What was original in Wagner's theory was his conception of the organizing principle of the music. An individual number or a concerted passage would no longer provide the sole structure for the music; rather, each act would be a single musical structure, comprised mainly of themes that recurred throughout the opera. These themes, which could be musical fragments or phrases or sometimes fully developed melodies, became associated with "a particular character, object, emotion, or concept" that had a crucial function in the action.[3] Once the audience associated these themes with their referents, their attention would be drawn to the most vital elements in the unfolding drama. Musical themes, combined with the words of the poem and the staging, would thus become the major medium through which the drama is expressed. This technique, later labeled the leitmotif or "leading motif" technique, brings to the fore the motivations that drive the action and the major thematic issues involved. Since this approach led to a sense of drama more heightened and specific than in conventional opera, Wagner would later insist that he was writing "music drama" as distinct from "opera," which for him by definition meant a noncontinuous musical stage work divided into numbers.

The Flying Dutchman does not provide the first instance of leitmotif in Wagner's works. The technique exists in primitive form in *The Ban on Love*, where a few leitmotifs are overused to the point of tedium. Furthermore, in contrast with the later works, where a large number of leitmotifs are employed with dizzying complexity, *The Flying Dutchman* has very few. Still, the simplicity and freshness with which the technique is applied makes it an ideal work to demonstrate its basic function. For example, there are two main leitmotifs associated with the leading characters. The overture opens with a leaping phrase, played mainly by the brass, expressive of rebellion and despair. In the course of the action, this leitmotif becomes associated with the Dutchman himself. In striking contrast, the second leitmotif, first played on the woodwinds, is calm and harmonious; in the course of the action, this will become associated with Senta and the salvation she brings the Dutchman. During the overture, which also contains leitmotifs associated with stormy weather, suffering, and the rough life of the sailors, Senta's leitmotif softens the Dutchman's. The overture ends with a triumphant combination of the two leitmotifs, anticipating the apotheosis at the end of the opera. The two leitmotifs are heard throughout the action; the Dutchman's sounds quietly in the orchestra when he first comes ashore and acquires great power toward the end of his entrance aria. Later, the leitmotif is heard whenever the Dutchman appears in someone's thoughts and, in the final scene of the opera, it is sung by his ghostly crew when they mock the terrified Norwegian sailors. Senta's redemption leitmotif first occurs in the dramatic action when she contemplates the picture of the Dutchman in the second scene, and the theme reappears each time Wagner wishes to draw attention to her function as the Dutchman's savior. Often the two leitmotifs are heard in conjunction, most splendidly at the end as a representation of the victory of Senta's love.

The potential of the leitmotif as a flexible dramatic language was far from fully realized in *The Flying Dutchman*. Furthermore, while Wagner claimed that the music was continuous, it is still possible to discern the discrete "numbers" method of composition characteristic of traditional opera. Nevertheless, this romantic opera represents an important step toward his achievement of a mature "music drama" in which music would be formed into a dramatic language unprecedented both in its flexibility and precision.

NOTES

1. Heinrich Heine, "Über die französische Bühne," *Werke*, ed. Eberhard Galley. 4 vols. (Frankfurt: Insel, 1968) 3: 253.

2. Attila Csampai and Dietmar Holland, eds., *Der fliegende Holländer: Texte, Materialien, Kommentare* (Hamburg: Ricordi, 1982), 103.

3. Barry Millington. *Wagner* (London: Dent, 1984), 127.

Chapter 3

Kapellmeister in Dresden

Before starting composition on *The Flying Dutchman*, Wagner had sent the score of *Rienzi* to the Dresden Court Theatre, hoping that an accompanying letter of recommendation from Meyerbeer would win the opera's acceptance. For once, his hopes were not disappointed. In June 1841, the Dresden management agreed to produce the opera sometime in the next year. Thus, in April 1842, Wagner's fortunes in Paris having improved not one whit, he and Minna determined to travel to Dresden, as only there did they seem to have some chance of a future. The welcome they received in Dresden, however, was not encouraging. Minna's family was too poor to put them up, so they had to find their own expensive accommodations. Moreover, the advent of the young composer embarrassed the theatre management who, whatever their official commitments, were not very enthusiastic about *Rienzi*, whose production date they kept postponing. An abortive trip to Berlin, where Wagner hoped to have *The Flying Dutchman* produced, only intensified the bleakness of the homecoming. All the same, the acceptance of *Rienzi* by the Dresden Court Theatre increased Wagner's standing in his family's eyes, so, at the instigation of his brother-in-law, Hermann Brockhaus (then professor of Oriental languages at Leipzig University), various family members paid him a modest allowance until royalties from the opera started coming up.

Persistence was one of Wagner's virtues. When the two major singers of the Dresden Opera, Wilhelmine Schröder-Devrient, the idol of his youth, and the heroic tenor Joseph Tichatschek returned to town in July, he insisted rehearsals begin. This bold move paid off, for over the next few months the soloists and company alike developed such enthusiasm for *Rienzi* that its success seemed assured. When eventually it was premiered on 20 October 1842 (Illustration 2), Wagner enjoyed one of the most triumphant nights of his entire career, an occasion that marked his institution in the public eye as a composer of considerable significance.

The success of *Rienzi* with the Dresden public and its subsequent enthronement as a centerpiece of the Court Theatre's repertoire are not surprising. The grandiose spectacle, vast ensembles, and heroic scenes of confrontation suggested that Germany had found another Meyerbeer in Wagner. But the now-famous young composer was far from elated. He experienced the first night as if it were a dream: "I felt no actual joy or emotion," he wrote later, "I seemed to be a stranger to my work" (*ML*, II, 20). He was apparently indifferent to the audience's cheers. His diffidence arose from his awareness that *Rienzi* represented neither his best nor his most personal work. With the experience of writing *The Flying Dutchman* already behind him, he knew how far the production of *Rienzi*, in which a Dance of Gladiators received the loudest applause, was from his ideal of music theatre: "I became increasingly aware," he wrote, "of the specific divergence between my inner aspirations and my outer success" (*ML*, II, 38). The production was designed from stock, as was customary, with no attention paid to realizing the character of the music visually, even though Wagner, while still in Paris, had urged that special scenery be designed so that the stage presentation should complement what he sensed to be unique in the work (*SB*, I, 587). All in all, Wagner experienced acute discomfort at seeing his opera placed on public display in Dresden.

His discomfort was intensified only two months later. The success of *Rienzi* was so great that the Dresden management determined to capitalize on it by acquiring the rights of *The Flying Dutchman* from the Berlin opera. But the première of the latter work on 2 January 1843 was a grave disappointment for the Dresden audience as well as for Wagner, leading him to realize "the special care that is needed to ensure the adequate dramatic interpretation of my latest works" (*ML*, II, 35). The main problem lay with the singers. Neither Schröder-Devrient as Senta nor the resident baritone Michael Wächter as the Dutchman was effective. Wächter, in particular, failed to understand the gloomy, introverted character of the Dutchman, so the personal crisis that is the main action of the opera went unrecognized. The stage presentation did nothing to help. Wagner saw the natural world as represented in the setting as a metaphor for the torment experienced by the Dutchman, but, oblivious to this, the Dresden management as usual cobbled the production together from sets used for other operas. Likewise, in the following year, when *The Flying Dutchman* was

Illustration 2. Closing scene of act 4 of *Rienzi*, Dresden, 20 October 1842. (From a woodcut in the *Leipziger Illustrierten Zeitung*. Reproduced by permission of the Nationalarchiv der Richard-Wagner-Stiftung/Richard-Wagner-Gedenkstätte, Bayreuth.)

produced in Berlin, the sets were borrowed from current productions of Weber's *Oberon*, Goethe's *Faust*, Rossini's *William Tell*, and other contemporary plays and ballets.[1] Under such circumstances, there was little chance that the stage could even approximate Wagner's personal vision.

Despite the failure of *The Flying Dutchman*—it was given only four times in Dresden, then dropped for twenty-five years—*Rienzi* kept Wagner in the public eye. Fortuitously, within five weeks of the first performance of *Rienzi*, both the Italian Kapellmeister and the music director of the Dresden theatre died, leaving a serious vacuum in the city's artistic leadership. Karl Reissiger, an easy-going, conservative conductor, was appointed to one position, and, somewhat predictably, Wagner, the celebrity of the moment, was offered the other. His feelings were intensely ambivalent. On the one hand, he was unwilling to accept the post, for he was acutely aware of the gap between his ambitions for the operatic stage and the actuality of stock productions and slovenly performance; more importantly, he feared that the duties of the appointment would interfere with his work as a composer. On the other hand, the regular salary of 1,500 thalers a year would be greatly welcome, burdened as he was with ever-increasing debts. Moreover, while the Dresden Opera was not so prestigious as its counterparts in Berlin and Vienna, it was unusual for a man with such limited experience as Wagner to be offered such a prominent position. Eventually, practical considerations won out, aided no doubt by the appeals of Minna, who welcomed a modicum of affluence and social respect after the hardships of Paris (Illustration 3). So, on 2 February 1843, Wagner received the permanent appointment of Royal Kapellmeister at the Dresden Court Opera.

The following six years represent the only period in Wagner's lifetime when he tried to create a permanent opera company that lived up to his own exacting standards within the conventional theatre. That he failed is due partly to his own volatility and egoism, partly to the laziness of his colleagues, and partly to the theatrical conditions of the time. Nevertheless, his achievement in Dresden was far from negligible, suggesting that, had events turned out differently, he had it within him to become one of the great musical and theatrical directors of the nineteenth century. In everything he did, he was impelled by a vision of theatre as "a temple in which all that was best in humanity was . . . put to uses as noble, as uplifting, as those of any temple devoted to the exercise of religion."[2] His ambitions, however, conflicted directly with those of most of the people with whom he had to work, including the world-weary Reissiger, whose main interest was the pension that he would collect at the end of his service, a concern that was apparently shared by most of the theatre's musical personnel. In

Illustration 3. Minna Wagner during the Dresden years. (Reproduced by permission of the Nationalarchiv der Richard-Wagner-Stiftung/Richard-Wagner-Gedenkstätte, Bayreuth.)

addition, Wagner did not get on well with the administration of the theatre, which, under the benign though not especially inspiring leadership of Baron von Lüttichau, a close friend of King Friedrich August II, was concerned mainly to provide the court with unchallenging entertainment. That the theatre could become the central institution of a society, in which values might be generated and transcendent experiences created, was a conception that Lüttichau's conventional thinking could never understand.

The conditions that Wagner encountered in Dresden were symptomatic of the wider German theatre of the time. The forty years spanning the turn of the eighteenth into the nineteenth century had seen a quite extraordinary growth of German theatre, from being a loose affiliation of traveling players, who performed under only the most primitive and improvised of circumstances, to a network of municipal, court, and national theatres that was more extensive and better subsidized than anywhere else in the world. During this period of growth, many of the classic dramas of the German theatre, by Gotthold Lessing, Goethe, Schiller, and Heinrich von Kleist, were written and, in all cases but Kleist's, were performed throughout Germany. In the realm of opera, the classic repertoire was founded on the work of Christoph Willibald Gluck, Mozart, Beethoven, and Weber. This was also an era noted for the vigor of its acting and for the widespread enthusiasm of the public for the theatre. By the early 1840s, however, much of this vitality had waned.

No doubt the decline was in part an inevitable reaction to several decades of vigorous growth, but it had political causes as well. The theatre in Germany was distinguished from theatre elsewhere in Europe as an institution in which the cultivation of the audience as citizens, as members of society, and as morally sentient beings was a clearly articulated aim. While this gave theatre great salience, this situation also made it more politically sensitive than its European counterparts and therefore more subject to governmental regulation. The repressive political conditions of post-Napoleonic Germany were characterized by the notorious Karlsbad Decrees of 1819, which attempted to control all education systems, quell all supposedly seditious writings, and suppress any opposition to the *status quo*. Imposed by means appropriate only to a police state, the decrees produced a quiescent culture quite unable to confront the major issues of its time. The only vital literature and drama were produced by the Young Germany movement of the 1830s, a loosely associated group of writers, some of whom, including Wagner's erstwhile friend Heinrich Laube, endured brief spells in prison on suspicion of subversion. Few of the plays of Young Germany reached the stage until the late 1840s. Under such conditions, theatre could hardly flourish as an effective force in German society.

In his great *History of German Acting*, Eduard Devrient, actor, director, and colleague of Wagner's during his days in Dresden, attributed the malaise primarily to a shift in the power structure of the theatre. Earlier in the century, during the heady days of expansion, theatre had been directed by actors intimately acquainted with the actualities of performance and with a knowledge of and concern for the repertoire. After 1815, however, as royal governments attempted to strengthen their hold on the theatres, intendants (managing directors) were appointed, not for their knowledge of the art but for their loyalty to the regime. Consequently, bureaucratic and political interests became the uppermost concerns in the day-to-day running of theatres, in the formulation of policy, and in the choice of repertoire, leading to what Devrient identified as widespread artistic demoralization.[3] The Dresden Court Theatre was no exception to this rule, Lüttichau having been an official in the Saxon Ministry of Forestry prior to his appointment as intendant.

According to Devrient, one of the most pernicious effects of this bureaucratization was the elevation of the virtuoso performer to a position of preeminence. The theatre has never lacked for egotists—indeed, when Wagner was still a child, E.T.A. Hoffmann, himself a theatre director of some repute, published a classic account of how the vanity of individual performers could destroy the integrity and coherence of any production.[4] Still, the lack of any controlling artistic presence in the 1830s and 1840s allowed for the development of individual performers concerned more with the display of virtuoso vocal skills and physical beauty than with the quality, texture, and substance of the work they were performing. With the exception of the Düsseldorf theatre, under Karl Leberecht Immermann in the 1830s, and the Vienna Burgtheater, ensemble performance was virtually unheard of in German-speaking Europe. Indeed, by the time Wagner arrived in Dresden, the Court Theatre there was celebrated as a center of virtuosity, with the star of its acting company being the most famous virtuoso of his day, the elegant classical actor Emil Devrient, Eduard's brother. Furthermore, until Wagner's appointment, Dresden was known as the German center for the performance of Italian opera, where singers were actively encouraged to display their vocal prowess. All these factors created a mode and ethos of performance more characteristic of the French theatre, as Wagner had described it in his essays from Paris, than of his ideal German theatre.

The size of the repertoire also stood in the way of achieving sustained artistic excellence. High quality in theatrical production depends substantially on performers having the opportunity to repeat their work in front of several, different audiences. Among the cities of German-speaking Europe only Berlin and Vienna were large enough to provide sufficiently large potential audiences to justify running a play or opera for several performances and even in those cities theatrical runs were the exception rather than the rule. In cities the size of Dresden and smaller, the repertoire had to be changed constantly in order to attract large enough audiences to keep the auditorium respectably full. Thus, in contrast to theatres in the twentieth century, German theatres of the nineteenth century put on a staggering number of performances of different plays and operas. Most theatres would not be open every day; in Leipzig, for example, during Wagner's youth, there were between 200 and 250 performances a year.[5] One out of every eight to ten evenings at the theatre would probably be a first night. For example, in 1844, the first complete calendar year in which Wagner severed as Kapellmeister in the Dresden Court Theatre, three tragedies, four dramas, nine comedies, and thirteen operas and musical plays were given new productions, a total of twenty-nine works in all. Some of these, like Karl Ferdinand Gutzkow's comedy *Zopf und Schwert* (*Pigtail and Sword*), *A Midsummer Night's Dream* in Ludwig Tieck's popular version with Mendelssohn's music, or Gaetano Donizetti's comic opera *The Daughter of the Regiment*, were repeated several times over the following years, but most productions were given only a handful of times and then dropped from the repertoire.[6] Under these circumstances, it was rarely possible to create a production in which all theatrical elements worked to complement each other. The handful of rehearsals given to most productions allowed for only the most rudimentary preparation. Performers rarely had the opportunity to study their roles at leisure, let alone to learn more than the most elementary blocking. Not surprisingly, the prompter, placed in his box in the center of the footlights, was one of the busiest people in the theatre. Such a bewilderingly rapid rate of production also meant that almost every piece was staged using stock scenery. Under such conditions, the modern concept of the stage set as a metaphor for inner action, an idea Wagner had hit upon in composing *The Flying Dutchman*, was quite impossible to realize.

That Wagner's initial doubts about the integrity of the German theatrical enterprise were strengthened in the course of his Dresden tenure is clear from two documents he wrote recommending fundamental changes in the structure of the Dresden Court Theatre and, by implication, of all theatrical activity in Saxony. The first of these papers focused exclusively on musical matters, proposing radical improvements in pay and working conditions for the orchestra and major changes in the configuration of instruments in the orchestra pit. This proposal was submitted in March 1846 and rejected by the administration a year later. The second paper, entitled "Draft of a Plan for a German National Theatre for the Kingdom of Saxony," concentrated more on specifically theatrical issues. Submitted to the administration on 16 May 1848, it was rejected out of hand, a clear indication of the growing gap between Wagner's ideas and those of the authorities.

The administrative structure that Wagner envisaged in the "Plan" challenged the hierarchy common in all German court theatres of the time by denying the court any control over artistic matters and placing final responsibility for the theatre in the hands of a "Ministry of Culture." He proposed that direct administration of the theatre be assigned to two committees, often working jointly. The first, appointed by a "Union of Dramatic Poets and Composers," would preserve standards by ensuring that only the finest work be produced and that all presentations "as far as possible be purged of the imperfections of experimental speculation" (*GSB*, XII, 108). The second committee, which represented stage personnel, would be responsible for pensions and welfare. A jury drawn from both committees would determine the repertoire. The general director would be elected for life by the union and the stage personnel. In addition to these administrative matters, Wagner went into details about a second national theatre in Leipzig, the elimination of traveling companies, the establishment of a training school for actors (at that time, there was none in Germany), and, crucially, given the very large repertoire of the time, a reduction in the number of performances of both plays and operas so that artistic standards might be raised. The plan included further detailed schemes for the utilization of the theatre orchestra.

Since the plan was written in 1848, it is not surprising that the royal government of Saxony, which was beginning to fear for its very existence, turned it down. But viewed in historical perspective and leaving aside the changes proposed in administration, the proposal is not so revolutionary as it may have seemed at the time. Nowhere in the document did Wagner challenge the characteristic German conception of theatre as an institution that guarantees the cohesiveness of the social body and furthers the education and cultivation of well-mannered citizens. In the preamble, he legitimized his plans by quoting no less an authority than the Hapsburg Emperor Josef II: "The Theatre should have no other duty, than to effect the refinement of taste and manners" (*GSB*, XII, 106–107). It was upon this assumption that Josef himself had founded the Vienna Burgtheater in 1776 and that a few decades later Goethe had trained his actors at the Weimar Court Theatre; both institutions still served in the 1840s as paradigms for German court theatre. Admittedly, Wagner's description of theatre as an autonomous institution working with "the full, free participation of the intellectual and moral forces of the nation" (*GSB*, XII, 107) might have sounded potentially subversive to the governmental *status quo*, but, in its specifically aesthetic purpose, the plan was conservative, in spirit far from the anarchy that was to break out on the streets of Dresden in May 1849.

Wagner's personal conduct, however, was enough to terrify any colleague or superior who feared insurrection. A man incapable of compromise, he was so possessed by his vision of the artistic potential of any project in which he was engaged that all other considerations had to be sacrificed to it. His defenders, of whom there have been many, have seen this as evidence that he was an artist of impeccable integrity; his detractors, of whom there have probably been an equally large number, have considered it indicative of ruthless egomania. There can be no doubt that Wagner's fury at being checked so frequently by the lethargy or obstinacy of others earned him innumerable enemies. This situation intensified the hatred of the conventional theatre that had been with him from his earliest years as a conductor. For example, in 1847, he engaged in an unpleasant power struggle with Gutzkow, the theatre's dramaturg for the spoken drama, who also wished to influence the performance and selection of operas. After intemperately denouncing Gutzkow to Lüttichau as an "evil genius, who through intrigues and insinuations destroys all mutual trust and leads our institution into certain moral decline" (*SB*, II, 551), Wagner wrote to a friend that he despaired at ever achieving anything in the theatre.

> I am so full of the deepest contempt for present conditions in the theatre, that as long as I feel I am not able to improve them, I have no stronger wish than to withdraw entirely, and regard it as a genuine curse that my whole creative urge is centered on the dramatic form, because I must recognize in the miserable conditions of our theatre nothing but the most complete contempt for my endeavors.[7]

Such complaints became increasingly frequent during his tenure as Kapellmeister. He was appalled at the "triviality and utter hopelessness" (*ML*, II, 165) he considered characteristic of all contemporary theatre.

The slowness with which his reputation was spreading in Germany intensified his pessimism. The promise of instant fame offered by the success of *Rienzi* in Dresden had evaporated. The sheer size of the opera—in all practicality, two evenings were required to perform it complete—and the reputation it quickly acquired for unduly straining the voices of singers meant that it was not taken up quickly by other German houses. A performance in Hamburg in March 1844 under Wagner's baton failed to impress, due to the inadequacies of the singers and a sloppy production; beyond that, it was seen only in Königsberg and Berlin in the 1840s. Even in Dresden, performance statistics indicate that it was not given as frequently as either *Der Freischütz* or Meyerbeer's operas. *The Flying Dutchman* fared only marginally better. It was given in Riga in May 1843 and in Cassel the following month in an excellent production. The latter was conducted by the aging composer Louis Spohr, who considered the music to be eminently singable and demonstrating much imagination and nobility of feeling.[8] In January 1844, the opera was given in Berlin; even though it was popular with audiences there, a hostile critical reaction, led by the city's leading critic Ludwig Rellstab, killed it. Wagner's next opera, *Tannhäuser*, had a mixed reception as its première in Dresden in October 1845, but soon won the favor of audiences. Soon it was as popular as *Rienzi*, even though its first performance outside Dresden took place only on 16 February 1849, in Weimar, under the direction of Franz Liszt. The dissemination of Wagner's operas was being hindered, it appeared, by their reputation as being difficult to stage and perform and by a constantly hostile press, which assured potential audiences, even before they heard the music, that they would not enjoy it.

Nevertheless, Wagner's work did not meet with total incomprehension. His skills as a musician and composer were readily recognized and, despite opposition from the more slothful members of the Dresden orchestra, standards improved markedly during his tenure at the theatre. Not ony did he rehearse and perform the popular works of Luigi Cherubini, Marschner, Meyerbeer, Rossini, and Weber, but he also explored the less familiar corners of the classic repertoire. Notable were his revivals of two rarely seen Gluck operas, *Armide* on 5 March 1843 and *Iphigenia in Aulis* on 22 February 1847, the latter in his own performing version, which remained standard in Germany for well over a century. Such accomplishments were not, however, achieved without friction. In particular, Wagner's style of conducting, in which he paid more attention to dynamics and phrasing than to overall structure, caused offense among colleagues.[9] Only a few months after his appointment, he had a major confrontation with Karl Lipinski, the leader of the orchestra, over his unorthodox interpretation of Mozart's *Don Giovanni*.

Still, Wagner began to acquire a following. The ardor he felt for his art was infectious. Among his colleagues in the theatre, August Röckel, an assistant conductor and political radical, and Theodor Uhlig, a violinist, became close personal friends. Outside the theatre, Wagner was prominent in the intellectual life of the city. Among his several acquaintances from café society were the poet and novelist Berthold Auerbach, several painters and sculptors, including the noted Julius Schnorr von Carolsfeld, and Gottfried Semper, architect of the new Dresden opera house that opened shortly before the arrival of Wagner. Toward the end of his time in Dresden, the young composer and conductor Hans von Bülow first heard Wagner's music and became fanatically attached to both Wagner and his music. Wagner even earned the grudging and occasionally bewildered respect of some highly notable musical figures. Berlioz visited Dresden soon after Wagner's arrival there and in his *Memoirs* acknowledged the help he received from Wagner during rehearsals, finding him to be "a figure of unusual interest and ability" whose works showed considerable promise.[10] Meyerbeer, whose intervention had been largely responsible for the acceptance of *Rienzi* in Dresden and *The Flying Dutchman* in Berlin occasionally referred warmly to the work of his protégé in his letters. Possibly out of envy of Meyerbeer's success and a growing sense of the imperfections of his operas, not to mention his increasing anti-Semitism, Wagner tried to distance himself from Meyerbeer's patronage, expressing only guarded respect in his public pronouncements and outright contempt in anonymous reviews and letters. His relationships with Mendelssohn, then conductor of the Leipzig Gewandhaus Orchestra, and with Robert Schumann, who lived in Dresden during the 1840s, were lukewarm. While both composers acknowledged Wagner's originality, neither was prepared to see in his music the greatness he was convinced it possessed. Like several others, they considered him little more than an oddly talented young man. Among established composers, only Liszt, whom Wagner had first met in Paris, sensed his potential greatness. Through a series of meetings in Dresden, the two men grew increasingly close, which led to Liszt's becoming the main champion of Wagner's music after the latter was deprived of all means of personally producing his work following the revolution of 1849.

Wagner's reputation for unorthodox behavior was no doubt heightened by the massive debts that he continued to amass throughout his time in Dresden. Unfortunately for him, the fame of *Rienzi* and his appointment as Kapellmeister brought down upon his head myriad demands for repayment from creditors stretching back to his Magdeburg days. His salary was simply not large enough to accommodate them all, and royalty payments for *Rienzi* were nonexistent after the first performance, for which he had been paid a mere 300 thalers. While he managed to pay off several more pressing debts, especially debts of honor owed to friends in Paris, he could not satisfy everybody. His parlous financial situation was aggravated too by his growing taste for luxury. As befitted his professional status, in October 1843 he and Minna moved into an expensive apartment in the Ostra-Allee in the center of the city, close to the theatre. This he not only furnished with great extravagance, but he also housed within it the considerable library he was in the process of accumulating. Roughly four years later, in October 1847, the couple had to move to a cheaper apartment in the suburbs, due to Wagner's deteriorating financial situation, caused partly by his unwise speculation. In the expectation that his music would soon be played throughout Germany, Wagner had printed, at his own expense, the full scores of *Rienzi*, *The Flying Dutchman*, and *Tannhäuser*, a project made possible through various loans, especially from Anton Pusinelli, a doctor who remained a lifelong friend, and a promise of money from Schröder-Devrient. The latter loan did not come through, however, since the singer's current lover forbade her to lend the money after the project was well underway. Wagner sent the published scores to all the major German opera houses, and almost all were returned; the package sent to Munich was not even opened. This substantial investment was entirely wasted, and it took Wagner over thirty years to pay it off. So extreme were his debts in the fall of 1846 that he appealed to Lüttichau for a raise in salary. He was granted part of what he requested and was extended a loan of 5,000 thalers from the theatre's pension fund. The loan tied him closely to the theatre and required him to practice extreme fiscal constraint, a discipline to which he could never subject himself. When he fled from Dresden in 1849, he may have owed as much as 20,000 thalers (*NLRW*, I, 508)—well over ten times his total annual salary. Wagner's debts, which were to be one of the major torments of his life, were already unpayable. The man was an irredeemable bankrupt.

Given the inordinate stresses that his debts and professional intrigues must have exercised on his peace of mind, it is remarkable that Wagner was capable of any creative work, but he had the enviable capacity to escape completely from the actual world into a more congenial one created by his imagination. Hence, amidst all his activity in Dresden, he created two operas that would eventually provide the basis for the spread of his fame throughout Germany and later Europe—*Tannhäuser*, which received its première in Dresden on 19 October 1845, and *Lohengrin*, first produced in Weimar on 28 August 1850.

Thematically, both works are closely related to *The Flying Dutchman*, for both focus upon the dilemma of the outsider. The fates of their protagonists can be regarded as projections of Wagner's perception of his own destiny in a society that he considered fundamentally unsympathetic to his aims. Tannhäuser is explicitly an artist, and the opera centers on the impossibility of reconciling the volatile nature of the artist and the mediocre world in which he is forced to live. The status of Lohengrin as an artist is more questionable, although Wagner's extensive commentary on the opera, which can be found mainly in the autobiographical essay "A Communication to My Friends" (1851), encourages such an interpretation (*GSB*, I, 123–131). The two operas are also linked to *The Flying Dutchman* by the recurring figure of a woman who is prepared to sacrifice all to guarantee the salvation of the man she loves.

The essentially personal issues at the heart of these works were exceptional in their time. With the wisdom of hindsight, we can see that Wagner's ambitions were unique as he began to use the medium of opera to explore the very experiences that constituted his own creativity. The use of the theatre as a means of self-discovery was not to become a mainstream endeavor among serious playwrights until late in the nineteenth century, with the work of Henrik Ibsen, August Strindberg, and those who followed them. This personal dimension to Wagner's work has been called "expressionist" (*BeRW*, 1–58), as if to identify its peculiar modernity.

Rienzi had succeeded by incorporating several of the most popular features of grand opera, while *The Flying Dutchman* had failed when it abandoned them. But while Wagner seized every opportunity to express his scorn for grand opera's obsession with external effect, he was not above exploiting this aspect of the genre for his own ends. Grand opera dealt mainly with public issues. He did not eschew these, but rather he incorporated them, in order to use the apparatus of grand opera to encompass themes that were intrinsically personal. Indeed, in addition to their musical splendors, *Tannhäuser* and *Lohengrin* may be considered to represent the supreme achievement of grand opera in the first half of the nineteenth century precisely because their action is metaphorical for a compelling personal crisis.

Both operas are drawn from the history and legends of Germany in the early Middle Ages. This choice in itself affirmed popular taste, for that period had engaged the interest of romantic writers and appealed widely to the reading public. Wagner's interest in the period went back to his days in Paris, where he had indulged his nostalgia for his homeland with readings from German history. *Tannhäuser* is based on the legendary Singers' Competition in the hilltop castle of the Wartburg, an event Wagner first encountered in Hoffmann's story *Der Kampf der Sänger* (*The Battle of Singers*), and, on the journey to Dresden, Wagner had passed the Wartburg, which reignited his interest. The idea of the opera became a consuming passion, however, only when, after reading Tieck's *Der*

Getreue Eckbart und der Tannhäuser (*Faithful Eckbart and Tannhäuser*),
he decided to combine the two separate legends.

Tannhäuser has both a mythical and historical setting. The minstrel
Tannhäuser has abandoned the world in order to indulge his senses at the
court of Venus in a grotto deep within the mountains. Yet he longs for a
purer world and escapes back to the Wartburg, seat of the Landgrave of
Thuringia, where, prior to his sojourn with Venus, he used to enchant
audiences with his songs. Elizabeth, the Landgrave's niece, has pined since
his departure, but she is filled with joy when he returns. In the song contest
that celebrates Tannhäuser's return, however, each minstrel describes the
joys of love and Tannhäuser creates a scandal by praising the physical
delights of Venus above those of a chaster love. He is rejected by the
Landgrave's court and in penance embarks on a pilgrimage to Rome; there
he receives the anathema rather than the blessing of the Pope. A broken
man, he returns to the Wartburg and dies, but not before he is saved by the
death of Elizabeth, whose soul will intercede for his. Tannhäuser's salvation is symbolized by the miracle of a wooden staff bursting into leaf.

The action centers upon the restless soul of the artist who is drawn from
one extreme to the other. As the artist is absorbed wholly by whatever
extreme state of mind possesses him, he is a highly contradictory figure.
"Tannhäuser," Wagner wrote, "is never and nowhere only 'a little' of
anything, but everything fully and entirely" (*GSB*, IX, 37). This fullness
both drives him to artistic expression and isolates him from the social
world, represented by the Wartburg. In searching for alternative modes of
existence, he can find rest neither in the Wartburg's antithesis, the court
of Venus, nor in the physical denial demanded by religious devotion. Like
the Dutchman, he is a congenitally restless man.

It is a measure of the richness of *Tannhäuser* that, unlike other contemporary grand operas, it is impossible to encompass the whole work within
a single interpretation. In contrast to *The Flying Dutchman*, it has a greater
range of action, which invites interpretations extending beyond the fate of
a single character to implicate the conflict between Christianity and
paganism, between physical and spiritual love, and between the life of
comfortable conformity, as represented by the knights of the Wartburg,
and less conventional experiences, as embodied by Tannhäuser or the
ascetic Elizabeth.

Fully aware of the multiplicity of these issues, Wagner was again
concerned that the physical setting of the opera should accurately express
the dramatic action. In an essay on performing *Tannhäuser*, he argued that
his music could achieve meaning only through scenic realization; consequently, the régisseur, scene designer, and music director should work as

one. The physical production depends on the conventions of grand opera, but Wagner was concerned that the tendency of familiar theatrical routine to become mechanical, a problem endemic in contemporary opera production, should be avoided. For example, he insisted that the entry of the guests for the singing contest, a massive choral set-piece, must not have the usual symmetry of a stage procession. He gave detailed instructions as to how "that painful regularity of the customary marching order" must be avoided. "The more diverse and informal the groups of oncomers, divided into separate groups of family and friends, the more engaging the effect of the whole entry" (*GSB*, IX, 32). Wagner's rejection of routine was directed at renewing audience interest in staging, thereby fastening their attention upon the specific meaning of each aspect of the physical production.

The concern for theatrical values is reflected too in the instructions to the singers. He insisted that *Tannhäuser* should not be rehearsed, as most operas are, with attention being paid solely to the music. Rather, the successful performer must be a "player" first, a "singer" second.

That singer who is not capable of first reciting his "part" as a role in a play, with an expression that corresponds to the intention of the *poet*, will under no circumstances be able to sing it in correspondence with the intention of the *composer*, not to mention the representation of the character in general. (*GSB*, IX, 12)

In order that the actor-singer grasp the essence of the characters to be represented, Wagner recommended they rehearse by speaking the words alone before learning the music. He even recommended that the orchestra be provided with copies of the words, so that they too would be fully aware of how the music enhanced their meaning.

Wagner's instructions as to how *Tannhäuser* should be performed cannot be taken as a totally accurate reflection of his ideas while composing the opera, since they were written in 1852, some seven years after the first performance in Dresden. By this time, his view of the opera had been conditioned by the theoretical works he had written with a more advanced concept of music drama in mind. Nevertheless, while composing *Tannhäuser*, he was convinced that it was a major advance over his previous work. "I expect to make a real revolution with it," he wrote to a friend, "for I feel that I have approached my ideal with giant steps!"[11] The revolution was not quite as radical as he had expected. At its première in Dresden, *Tannhäuser* caused neither a great sensation nor a major scandal. Those parts written in the formal style of grand opera, such as the entry of the guests and the sextet in which Tannhäuser is banished, were successful.

Other passages did not instantly impress audiences, partially because Schröder-Devrient as Venus and Tichatschek as Tannhäuser were inadequate dramatically. While the tenor's stentorian tones were ideal for *Rienzi*, the subtleties of characterization that indicate the broken and distinctly unheroic mentality of Tannhäuser were beyond him. Wagner's niece Johanna as Elizabeth and Anton Mitterwurzer as Tannhäuser's friend Wolfram were more successful. The stage production was hardly adequate either. Although Lüttichau ordered new sets, which represented a sign of considerable respect, act 2 was still performed against a set designed for Weber's *Oberon*, with no attention paid to the specifics of staging.

Tannhäuser did not, however, remain long in obscurity. By the third performance, it had started to acquire a following and was soon almost as popular in Dresden as *Rienzi*. No doubt this was due in part to the music, which, in contrast to *The Flying Dutchman*, has the range and sheer size characteristic of grand opera. It also has a particular fervor, best described by Wagner himself, who recalled composing the opera in a stage of "burning, voluptuous excitement that kept my blood and nerves in feverish agitation" (*GSB*, I, 108). This is especially evident in the Venusberg scenes, in the dramatic confrontations of act 2, and in Tannhäuser's compelling final soliloquy as he describes his pilgrimage to Rome, the Pope's curse, and his miserable return. The impact of these passages is strengthened by strikingly contrasting sections that express the peace that can come through deep faith, in particular the Pilgrims' Chorus, much of Elizabeth's music, and Wolfram's celebrated aria, "O du, mein holder Abendstern" ("O star of eve"). Leitmotifs are here more prominent than in *The Flying Dutchman*. Most distinctive are the two contrasting melodies upon which the famous overture is built, a solemn tune played in the lower brass that becomes the great Pilgrims' Chorus and the frenzied whirling passages that describe the orgy in the Court of Venus. More developed than most leitmotifs, these consistently appear at appropriate points in the action to clarify the conflict and, in conjunction with other leitmotifs, express Tannhäuser's particular state of mind at various points in the action. Unlike Wagner's later use of leitmotif, the usage here is never retrospective but devoted to explaining present motivation.[12]

Listeners today can easily discern the formal numbers—arias, duets, choruses—and the extended melodies that identify *Tannhäuser* as grand opera but, to Wagner's contemporaries, they were not so apparent. After reading the score, Schumann complained to Mendelssohn that the music was no better than that in *Rienzi*: "really he cannot write four beautiful bars, let alone good bars one after the other." Schumann also attacked

Wagner's harmony and four-part choral writing. Interestingly, once he heard the opera in the theatre, his opinion changed entirely. The stage made sense of music that had previously seemed formless. Consequently, Schumann found *Tannhäuser* to be "a hundred times better than his earlier operas" and determined that Wagner "can be of great significance for the stage, and, as I know, he has the courage for it."[13]

If that courage was to involve the reform of the stage, Wagner's next opera did not demonstrate it. Instead, *Lohengrin* stands at a high point in the development of romantic grand opera, culminating a tradition rather than initiating new forms and modes of staging. The idea for *Lohengrin* had germinated during Wagner's reading for *Tannhäuser*, but he did not start working on it methodically until the summer of 1845 when, during a holiday supposedly taken to recuperate his health, he studied contemporary editions of the medieval myths of Parsifal, Titurel, and Lohengrin. The entire plot seems to have occurred to him with remarkable suddenness, suggesting that he had great confidence in the material. Certainly, the final version of the opera is unusually close to the initial prose scenario in which he wrote out the action of the opera in considerable detail.

Lohengrin has a specific historical setting—Antwerp in the year 933. King Henry the Fowler of Germany wishes to unite the Saxons and the Brabantians in battle against the Hungarians, but political discord threatens when a Brabantian count, Telramund, accuses Elsa, the daughter of the old Duke of Brabant, of murdering her younger brother Gottfried. Elsa's only defense is that her innocence will be proved by a knight who will come to save her. The knight appears miraculously in a boat drawn by a swan and defeats Telramund in single combat. He then agrees to lead the German troops in battle and promises to marry Elsa on condition that she never ask his name or origin. During the night before the wedding, Ortrud, Telramund's wife, gains Elsa's confidence and then uses it to undermine severely her faith in the knight by harping on her ignorance of his name. After a dramatic confrontation between Ortrud and Elsa on the way to the cathedral, Elsa overcomes her doubts sufficiently to marry him. On the wedding night, however, she cannot resist asking his name. As she does, Telramund breaks into the bedroom but is slain by the knight. The knight then announces to the king and his assembled troops that he must return to the realm from which he came. He states first the name of his father, Parsifal, and then his own, Lohengrin, revealing that he is a knight of the Grail. The swan reappears and miraculously turns into the child Gottfried, whom Elsa had been accused of killing. Lohengrin sails back to the land of the Grail, leaving Elsa lifeless in the arms of her brother.

More than *Tannhäuser*, *Lohengrin* has an uncomplicated grand-opera setting, with no attempt being made to use the stage as a metaphor for the mental state of the central figure. This simplicity is complemented by a rigorously structured plot in which the action unfolds with exceptional clarity. In fact, it is clear from *Lohengrin* that Wagner had mastered the conventional dramaturgy of the time more successfully than the generally accepted experts had. Most French grand operas were composed to libretti produced by noted practitioners of the well-made play, of whom Scribe was the most celebrated. Wagner's Parisian experience had, of course, prejudiced him against French opera, but the libretto—or "poem," as he preferred to call it—for *Lohengrin* is ironically a far more accomplished achievement, in terms of the well-made play, than any of Scribe's opera texts. Two of the most famous operas for which Scribe provided libretti, Auber's *Mute Girl of Portici* and Fromental Halévy's *La Juive* (*The Jewess*), are actually diffuse and lacking in momentum, as their plots stray into incidental issues and intrigues not germane to the action. Curiously, Wagner expressed some respect for both works. *Lohengrin*, in contrast, is strikingly cohesive. The pivotal secret of Lohengrin's name is crucial to the action, in contrast to the purely incidental interest of secrets in Scribe's operatic intrigues. Wagner's action is also more simple. Recognizing, as French librettists usually did not, that complex plotting is unsuited to opera, he stripped the action to its barest minimum, thereby allowing himself ample opportunity to explore the emotions of his characters.

For a composer and dramatist who has acquired a reputation for prolixity, *Lohengrin* demonstrates rigorous unity of action and a meticulous structuring of plot. Act 1 consists of a tripartite exposition leading up to the inciting moment of Lohengrin's entrance and his defense of Elsa. The first scene of act 2 reaches its climax as Ortrud insinuates her way into Elsa's entourage, a foreshadowing of the catastrophe to come, while the second scene, which includes some of the grandest choral passages in all opera, culminates magnificently in Elsa's anticipation of marital bliss being imperiled by the threats of Ortrud. The opening scene of act 3, in the bridal chamber, provides the crisis when Elsa asks the fatal question, while the final scene comprises an extended dénouement. Throughout, the music complements the progress of the action, each climactic moment of the plot being marked by a climax within the score. Moreover, the tightness of the plot invests the action with a sense of inevitability unusual even in Wagner's work. All in all, *Lohengrin* has a musical and dramatic coherence, a classical unity, unequaled in the grand opera of the time. Liszt rightly referred to it as "an indivisible wonder."[14]

The theme of the lonely artist and of the woman who sacrifices herself to save him is treated with greater objectivity than in the two previous operas. Wagner projected onto Lohengrin his conception of his own position as an artist isolated from the world by his idealism and yet longing for human contact through the unquestioning love of a woman. He claimed that not only did the situation apply directly to his own predicament—his marriage with Minna, though outwardly tranquil, was beginning to undergo considerable strain—but also that the impossibility of the union of Lohengrin and Elsa symbolized the fate of the artist in modern society. Hence, the myth of *Lohengrin* was to be taken as uniquely illustrative of the condition of the modern artist faced with an uncomprehending world (*GSB*, I, 123–31).

In fact, as Wagner came to realize later in his commentary on *Lohengrin*, sympathies are not distributed as one-sidedly as he initially suggested. Early in his work on the mythological material, he admitted that he was somewhat repelled by the Lohengrin figure, "who filled me with mistrust and that distinct repugnance that we feel when we look at the carved and painted saints and martyrs on the highways and in the churches of Catholic countries" (*GSB*, I, 117). Although the character eventually lost its Gothic trappings, an aura of coldness still surrounds him; in contrast to Tannhäuser, he maintains an unbroken, heroic demeanor, behind which only fleeting hints of tragic passion can be detected. In reaction to this impassivity, which aroused some negative criticism when Wagner first read the poem to his friends, a corresponding sympathy arises for Elsa, who, in contrast to Senta and Elizabeth, is a fully developed character with passions of her own. At the start of the opera, she, like the two earlier female characters, is prepared to obliterate her identity for that of her lover, but, as the action progresses, we come to recognize her right to know his name and identity, for only when she knows it will she possess him as completely as he wishes to possess her. It is Elsa who grows in the course of the action, and who, in her progress from innocent erotic dreamer to responsible and guilty adult, exercises the fullest hold on our sympathies. As a consequence, we view Lohengrin and the rights that he claims with an increasingly skeptical eye. For the first time, Wagner invested his action with a consistent irony, which makes the opera as much a self-indictment as a self-defense.

Although the personal dilemma of the artist's erotic fulfillment is at the core of the opera, it is not the only concern. Wagner conducted detailed research into Brabant in the tenth century and, with the historicist mentality characteristic of his time, was concerned to ensure that details of ceremonial and custom were reproduced on stage as accurately as possible.

This was not just to follow fashion, for it had an artistic purpose; namely, such physical exactitude was needed to ensure that the spiritual realm that Lohengrin represents stand out in strong contrast to the physical world. The broader implications of the conflict, between Lohengrin and Henry on one side and Ortrud and Telramund on the other, relate to the battle between a still nascent Christianity and a residual barbarism, which, Wagner argued, paralleled the contemporary struggle between liberal nationalism and the repressive conservative elements still in power. In addition, his interest in the historical background reflected his growing concern for German national issues. The character of King Henry articulates a vision of German unity not apparent in any of the rulers of German states contemporary to Wagner. The king is also an aptly symbolic figure that Wagner could exploit to define the difference between his concept of theatre and the gaudy show associated with French opera. He insisted that the opera be staged with attention to the sober, simple customs that marked Henry the Fowler's rule, in contrast to the gaudier "Franco-Byzantine" ceremonials that were introduced by the next generation. The stage would therefore make manifest the austerity that Wagner had conceived to be characteristic of German culture back in his Paris days.

It would, however, be difficult to justify such simplicity from the music. The most striking features of the score are the immense choruses during the bridal procession and the massing of warriors. These are anticipated by extended orchestral interludes that include spectacular trumpet calls and build to impressive climaxes. *Lohengrin*'s world is supremely that of grand opera, but not solely because of its noise and spectacle. The rarefied music of the Grail, heard first in the mysterious and haunting Prelude, embodies the metaphysical realm from which the hero comes. Such music has a magical effect when contrasted with the more vigorous tones of the earthly action. The one scene of intimacy between Lohengrin and Elsa in the bridal chamber consists mainly of a love duet written with Italianate lyricism, demonstrating Wagner's rich melodic gifts more effectively than any other music that he wrote at this period. But the most striking scene musically and dramatically comes at the beginning of act 2, when Ortrud, the one character wholly invented by Wagner (there being no precedents for her in his source material) first persuades Telramund to murder Lohengrin and then insinuates her way into Elsa's household. The leitmotif associated with her embodies perfectly her insidious influence and the baleful power of heathenism, which Wagner considered analogous to the destructive traits of desire for revenge and greed for possessions characteristic of society in his own time. The manner in which Ortrud's leitmotif intertwines with the music of the other characters, first with

Telramund's despair and then with Elsa's ecstatic contemplation of union with Lohengrin, which Ortrud will help to destroy, clearly anticipates the mature music drama that Wagner would embark upon during the 1850s.

NOTES

1. Oswald Georg Bauer, *The Stage Designs and Productions from the Premières to the Present*, trans. Peter Loeffler (Basel: Birkhäuser, 1982), 50 (henceforward, *BaRW*).

2. Ernest Newman, *The Life of Richard Wagner* 4 vols. (New York: Knopf, 1933–1946), I: 369 (henceforward *NLRW*).

3. Devrient, *Geschichte*, II, 186–197.

4. E.T.A. Hoffmann, *Seltsame Leiden eines Theater-Direktors*, ed. Hans-Joachim Kruse (Berlin: Aufbau, 1977), 357–473.

5. Oscar Fambach, *Das Repertorium des Stadttheaters zu Leipzig, 1817–1828* (Bonn: Bouvier, 1980).

6. Robert Prölss, *Geschichte des Hoftheaters zu Dresden* (Dresden: Baensch, 1878), 616–648.

7. *Richard Wagner's Briefe an Theodor Uhlig, Wilhelm Fischer, Ferdinand Heine* (Leipzig: Breitkopf & Härtel, 1888).

8. Csampai and Holland, eds., *Der fliegende Holländer*, 112–115.

9. Paul Bekker, *Richard Wagner: His Life in His Work*, trans. M. M. Bozeman (Freeport: Books Libraries, 1931), 143 (henceforward *BeRW*).

10. Hector Berlioz, *The Memoirs*, trans. David Cairns (London: Panther, 1970), 369.

11. *Letters of Richard Wagner: The Burrell Collection*, ed. John N. Burk (New York: Macmillan, 1950), 136.

12. Carl Dahlhaus, *Richard Wagner's Music Dramas*, trans. Mary Whittall (Cambridge: Cambridge University Press, 1980), 27–34.

13. Attila Csampai and Dietmar Holland, eds., *Tannhäuser: Texte, Materialien, Kommentare* (Hamburg: Ricordi, 1986), 121.

14. *Wagner-Liszt Briefwechsel*, I, 75 (*WLB*).

Chapter 4

Revolutionary in Exile

Between completing *Lohengrin* and starting composition on *The Ring of the Nibelungs*, a nexus of public revolution and private crisis occurred in Wagner's life that changed his whole career and his position not only in the German theatre, but in German society as a whole.

The Karlsbad Decrees of 1819 had created a society in which individual rights were limited, economic opportunities exceptionally confined, and constitutional development stunted. A series of minor risings in 1830 had indicated the fragility of absolutist government in the various German states, all of which were still nominally independent. Widespread protests throughout German-speaking Europe did not erupt until early in 1848. Then, ignited by the February Revolution in Paris that led to the abdication of the French king, insurrection in Vienna first toppled Prince Klement Wenzel Metternich and later caused the abdication of the Austrian emperor in favor of his nephew. These events led to demonstrations and occasionally violent riots in various German states, though only in Berlin was there any serious bloodshed. The upshot of these civil disturbances was the introduction of a number of democratic measures and liberal ministers in various local state governments. The most significant immediate outcome of the 1848 revolution in Germany was the establishment of a National Assembly in Frankfurt, composed primarily of professionals and intellectuals representing the several German states. Ideally, the Assembly would bring political unity to Germany and thereby weaken the power of autocratic royalist government in each of the states. As conservative reaction to the revolution strengthened in the latter half of 1848, however, the Assembly's power weakened, and it was forced to disband in March 1849.

Dresden, the capital of Saxony, was not directly affected by the uprisings of 1848. Nevertheless, revolutionary currents could be felt there, and Wagner, whose position at the Court Theatre was growing increasingly tenuous, became caught up in them, weakening his position in the theatre still more. In June 1848, soon after his plan for the reorganization of the theatre had been rejected, he delivered a speech to the left-wing *Vaterlandsverein* (Fatherland Society), advocating a combination of monarchy, republicanism, and aggressive German nationalism—a confusing mixture of conservative and radical ideas that indicates that he was never really party to any identifiable revolutionary cause or dogma. Soon after this, under the guise of a leave of absence for reasons of health, he traveled to Vienna, which was then in the throes of revolution. There he indulged in abortive plans to take over the management of the Kärntnertortheater and to reorganize the Viennese theatre in the cause of the revolution. On his return to Dresden, he found himself further isolated when he was passed over for a decoration that went to Reissiger, and, in December, he suffered the crowning insult when the Dresden management refused to stage *Lohengrin*. A few months later, Lüttichau would not even grant him leave to go to Weimar to attend the first production of *Tannhäuser* outside Dresden. Wagner was both an outcast and a prisoner of his own theatre.

These personal setbacks drew him into the escalating instability of the political situation in Saxony. Further risings had occurred in various parts of Germany due to the failure of the Frankfurt Assembly in March 1849. In Saxony, public pressure had forced the conservatively minded king to install a liberal government, and increasing divisions between the parliamentary Chamber of Deputies and the royal court threatened a breakdown in public order. The decline in Wagner's fortunes at the Dresden theatre paralleled this slide into public anarchy. His friend August Röckel was dismissed from the theatre orchestra for left-wing political activities, which included editing the radical newspaper *Volksblätter*. Then, early in 1849, Wagner made the acquaintance of the Russian insurrectionist Mikhail Bakunin, who was in Dresden to agitate rebellion and who actually hailed a performance of Beethoven's *Choral Symphony*, conducted by Wagner on Palm Sunday, as a harbinger of revolution. But unlike Bakunin, Wagner was never a systematic political thinker. He became involved in public rebellion for personal reasons and out of the quite impracticable belief that revolution would bring about conditions under which his art could flourish independent of commercial and institutional pressures. Nevertheless, his position in the revolutionary opposition became ever more apparent as he delivered inflammatory broadsides against the *status quo*. The most notable of these was an article entitled "The Revolution," which appeared in the *Volksblätter* on 8 April 1849, an ecstatic outburst describing the coming apocalypse in which all property would be destroyed, all inequities annulled, and the class system obliterated.

> I will destroy the existing order of things, which divides united mankind into hostile peoples, into powerful and weak, into privileged and outlawed, into rich and poor, as it makes all men *unhappy*. I will destroy the order of things that makes millions into the slaves of few and these few into slaves of their own power and wealth. (*GSB*, XII, 34)

In actuality, of course, no such cataclysm occurred. Civil discontent burst into rebellion when the King of Saxony dissolved the Chamber of Deputies on 30 April 1849. On 3 May, the king withdrew to his castle at Königstein, for there was fighting in the streets of Dresden. The next day, the revolutionaries formed a provisional government, but this was soon unseated by the arrival of Prussian troops, which had already aided in suppressing a series of revolutionary disturbances throughout the German states. Reinforced by the Saxon army, the Prussians had crushed all armed opposition by 9 May. Wagner's claim in his autobiography that he was not closely involved in these events is not to be trusted, mainly because he wrote the book at the request of a later royal patron, Ludwig II of Bavaria, and it is clear from letters and other documents that, while he was never a decision maker, he was close to the leadership of the rebellion. On the night of 5 May, he reported troop movements from the tower of the Kreuzkirche and acted as courier for the provisional government. Furthermore, after the opposition was crushed, he fled from Dresden to Chemnitz in the company of Bakunin and other ringleaders, escaping arrest quite by chance because he spent the night in a different inn than they did.

The police, however, were not prepared to let him go free. After the insurrection, 12,000 arrests were made. Among these was Röckel, who was found to be in possession of an incriminating letter from Wagner. Accordingly, a warrant was issued for Wagner's arrest on charges of high treason. He had escaped to Weimar, where he sought temporary shelter with Liszt, but was unable to remain there due to an extradition treaty among the German states. So, after a brief visit from Minna, acting on Liszt's advice, he determined to travel to Paris, where, safe from arrest, he could make arrangements to have his operas produced. On 24 May, he bade farewell to both Liszt and Minna, and, three days later, using a forged passport, he crossed the Bodensee to Switzerland and made his way to Zurich. It would be eleven years before he would return to Germany.

Through the good offices of Jakob Sulzer, a cantonal secretary in Zurich, Wagner obtained a Swiss passport that enabled him to travel to Paris, but his renewed contact with this most modern of metropolises filled him with disgust. In reaction, the idyllic landscape of Switzerland seemed a most attractive haven, and, within a week, he had returned to Zurich. Two months later, he was joined by Minna, and they proceeded to settle into the city that would be their home for the next nine years. The following spring, Wagner returned breifly to Paris in another attempt to arrange the production of his operas, but this came to nothing. Instead, he almost had an affair with Jessie Laussot, the English-born wife of a rich Bordeaux wine merchant, but this too proved fruitless, so in July a chastened Wagner returned to the domestic confines of Zurich.

Once he had settled down, Wagner's life in Zurich was outwardly peaceful and uneventful. He made no attempt to find permanent employment, since this would prevent him from devoting his full energies to creative work. But during his residence in Zurich, his fame as a composer and polemicist grew so rapidly that he became a celebrity in Germany, the very country from which he was exiled, and his fame made it impossible for him to refuse to participate to some extent in the circumscribed artistic life of Zurich. Toward the end of 1850, he began occasionally to conduct popular repertory pieces at the local opera house and, between January 1851 and March 1855, led twenty-two concerts of the local music society, a series that included three concerts devoted to his own music in the summer of 1853—in effect, the first "Wagner Festival." In the spring of 1855, soon after the first performance of *Tannhäuser* in Zurich, he left for London, hoping to earn a fortune by conducting a three-month season with the Philharmonic orchestra. This trip turned out to be a profoundly unhappy experience. While audiences were enthusiastic and he was even received by Queen Victoria (an event that he reported with considerable pride), the press was intensely hostile. Worst of all, Wagner found London, the most commercialized city in Europe, no less than a contemporary incarnation of Dante's Inferno (*WLB*, II, 73). The whole experience only intensified his hatred of modern urban life. Because the high cost of living in London consumed all of his hard-earned money, he did not even have the satisfaction of retreating to the paradise of Switzerland with a profit.

Not surprisingly, his finances improved little during the Zurich years. Although his operas were being performed with increasing frequency in Germany, he received minuscule amounts in payment, since there was no legal way in which he could extract royalty payments. Despite this, he achieved some financial stability, mainly through the good offices of Julie Ritter, a moderately well-off admirer, who granted him a small pension of 800 thalers per year; this was sufficient to take care of his and Minna's basic needs. But while he might inveigh against the luxury of contemporary civilization, Wagner was not the man to deny himself. In particular, when composing he insisted on working in opulent surroundings that gratified his senses, which made exorbitant demands on his straitened budget. Throughout the Zurich years, letters to friends such as Liszt and Pusinelli were peppered with urgent requests for financial aid. Luckily, even though his debts mounted, Wagner usually found patrons willing to help him, in particular, the German businessman Otto Wesendonk, who had settled in Zurich with his wife Mathilde after earning a fortune in the United States.

Wagner was a man of great energy, and, each summer in the first years of his stay in Zurich, he would take hikes through the Alps lasting several weeks. Nevertheless, it soon became clear that however much exercise he might take, he would never enjoy good health. His budget was, therefore, further strained by expensive medical treatments and cures. All the same, he continued to suffer ill health, although he did find a doctor able to cure him of erysipelas, a disfiguring skin disease that had plagued him since his youth. Minna was less fortunate; she began to display signs of serious heart trouble. But, despite the health problems, to a dispassionate observer Wagner's fortunes in Zurich might have seemed enviable. He was not living in abject poverty; he was accorded respect, even acclaim, by the local community; and he enjoyed the company of stimulating friends. Sulzer, the civil servant who had arranged his passport, was a constant companion, while he also enjoyed warm relationships with writers such as Georg Herwegh, the revolutionary poet, and the novelist Gottfried Keller. Their company was augmented in 1855 when Gottfried Semper, another refugee from the Dresden uprising, was appointed to a teaching position at the Zurich Polytechnic, mainly through Wagner's intercession.

During his time in Zurich, Wagner began to attract followers whose admiration for his work and fascination with his personality were so intense that they can be described as the first "Wagnerian" disciples. Among them were his patron Julie Ritter, her son Karl, and Hans von Bülow, who in later years would, as a conductor, be the first major interpreter of some of Wagner's greatest works. But Wagner probably felt closest to Liszt, who visited him in 1853 after a four-year separation. On this occasion, Liszt claimed that he behaved "something like a Vesuvius letting off fireworks, emitting sheaves of flame and bouquets of roses and lilacs" (*NLRW*, II, 385). The two men were totally compatible and at one in their admiration for each other's music. While the relationship later came under strain, particularly after 1856 when Liszt argued with Karl Ritter and Wagner found himself at odds with Liszt's aristocratic mistress, the two men remained artistic soulmates throughout their lives.

Despite appearances, however, Wagner was far from happy. As his stay in Zurich grew longer, he felt increasingly depressed and isolated. His letters suggest that he may even have considered suicide. As he wrote in a letter to Liszt:

> I live a perfect dream life here; when I awake, it is only with pain. Nothing charms or holds me—or—whatever charms and holds me— is in the distance. How shall I avoid falling into the deepest depression? . . . My nights are generally sleepless—I climb out of bed tired and miserable, seeing before me a day that will not bring me *one* joy! Spending time with people who only torture me and from whom I withdraw only in order to torture myself! I am disgusted at whatever I do.—It cannot go on like this! I may not bear life much longer! (*WLB*, I, 99)

His misery was caused in part by the provinciality of small-town life, for however much he abhorred big cities, only there could his artistic and intellectual energies be fully satisfied. He was also homesick for Germany. In 1852, an inquiry as to whether he might be granted amnesty was answered in the negative, and further pleas in 1854 and 1856 were also rejected.

The main reason for Wagner's distress at his exile was that it isolated him from his work. While he was forced to remain mainly within the confines of Switzerland, his operas were suddenly in demand throughout Germany. The success of *Tannhäuser* on the small stage of the Weimar Court Theatre in February 1849 had dispelled the opera's reputation as being unstageable and unperformable. Soon it was taken up by other houses, being given in 1852 at Schwerin, Breslau, and Wiesbaden, in 1853 at Leipzig and Cassel, and in 1855 at Hanover and Karlsruhe. All in all, forty different productions were staged in smaller German cities before Franz Dingelstedt, the controversial intendant of the Munich Court Theatre, gave it a major production in a lavish setting. Productions in Berlin and Vienna followed in 1856 and 1859 respectively (*BaRW*, 70–78). *Lohengrin* fared equally well. It received its première under Liszt's baton in Weimar on 28 August 1851, the one-hundred-first anniversary of Goethe's birth. By 1860, it had received twenty-one different productions in German-speaking cities, including Vienna in 1858 and

Berlin in 1959 (*BaRW*, 111–113). The recognition he was receiving did not, however, bring joy to Wagner. For a start, the very thought of his work being performed without any personal consultation with him was a torment, so much so that the first production of *Tannhäuser* in Berlin was considerably delayed, due to his insistence that only Liszt should supervise it and the unwillingness of the intendancy of the Royal Theatre to go along with this arrangement. So attached was Wagner to his work that even sympathetic criticism offended him. Soon after the successful première of *Tannhäuser* in 1845, he wrote to the critic Eduard Hanslick claiming that he experienced any criticism of his work as if the person reviewing it

> had grasped hold of my intestines in order to examine them . . . . for me a performance of my opera before an audience is a constant battle against such boundless inner agitation that there have often been times when, feeling myself incapable of the fight, I have tried to prevent performances from taking place. (*SB*, II, 535)

The most serious problem caused by Wagner's separation from his work was, quite simply, that he was unable to hear his music. Strangely, while tens, possibly even hundreds of thousands of Germans heard *Lohengrin* in the 1850s, the composer himself did not hear it until 1861. This delay was a distinct handicap since, however completely the music sounded in his inner ear, he needed the event of public performance to gauge the work's impact and to adapt it, as he had already adapted *The Flying Dutchman* and *Tannhäuser*, until it came as close as possible to satisfying him entirely.

Ultimately though, Wagner's inability to engage in unbroken work in a theatre while in Zurich had a positive impact on his career. For five years, between 28 April 1848, when he completed the score of *Lohengrin*, and 1 November 1853, when he began composition on *The Rhinegold*, the first of the *Ring* music dramas, he engaged in no sustained musical composition. While this inability to compose contributed substantially to the despair that often gripped him, his mind was far from inactive; on the contrary, this was a time of great intellectual ferment. Profoundly dissatisfied as he was with both the state of contemporary theatre and the mode and structure of grand opera, in a series of essays and books he formulated, methodically and down to the finest detail, the basic principles upon which his later music dramas were to be based—the works that would dominate the imagination of generations of later artists and audiences. In these writings, he began to expound a vision that led the European theatre to alter radically its understanding of both its artistic mission and its social function. So powerful were his ideas and so complete his achievement, that his enforced absence from theatre, however frustrating it might have been personally, must be regarded as beneficial, for it allowed him the liberty to meditate on the potential of theatre free from the restrictions of practice. These would reimpose themselves later.

The initial impetus for this writing came from his experiences on the barricades in Dresden. The excitement that the revolution aroused in him took several months to abate; in fact, the objectification of his rebellion against established authority came about only through his writing. The first two major essays, "Die Kunst und die Revolution" ("Art and Revolution") and "Das Kunstwerk der Zukunft" ("The Art-Work of the Future") were quickly completed and published in 1849. They were followed by his *magnum opus* in the field of theory, the immense *Oper und Drama* (*Opera and Drama*), published in November 1851. Other important essays, also published in 1851, included "Ein Theater in Zürich" ("A Theatre for Zurich"), which appeared in the influential German periodical *Neue Zeitschrift für Musik*, and the long autobiographical essay "Eine Mitteilung an meine Freunde" ("A Communication to my Friends"), a prefatory essay attached to an edition of the poems of *The Flying Dutchman*, *Tannhäuser*, and *Lohengrin*. These essays, combined with the copious letters that flowed from his pen, provide a rich record of his developing ideas on the social function of art, the nature of theatre, and his concept of the new form of music drama.

Wagner's literary work has a formidable reputation, which is not entirely undeserved. At its worst, his prose is florid, overwritten, and frequently incomprehensible. His version of the history of drama and opera is tendentious in the extreme, while his most influential theory of the *Gesamtkunstwerk*, or the total or comprehensive work of art, is far from original, having been the stock in trade of several theorists of the Romantic period and earlier.[1] Nevertheless, his contemporaries, accustomed to florid style and unfamiliar with the history of theatre, found his writing more compelling than we do today. This, combined with the crowning achievements of the music dramas that were to follow, ensured an enthusiastic readership and an influence that lasted well into the twentieth century.

Wagner's theoretical treatises were founded upon the same assumptions as the literary work he had completed in Paris ten years previously. According to him, modern civilization was fueled and disfigured by an overwhelming desire for material gain. In Wagner's imagination, this was symbolized above all by the oppressive city of Paris, where artistic undertakings were successful only to the extent that they could be exploited commercially. In his imagination, the antithesis to this was the small, semirural culture of Germany, which offered greater freedom to cultivate the inner life. His experience in Dresden, however, had taught him that the influence of commerce on art was not exclusive to France. Indeed, his anti-Semitism, which declared itself at this time in the notorious essay "Das Judentum in Musik" ("Jews in Music"), drove him to identify much of this modern concern with material gain with Jews, both within and outside Germany. What was needed, he claimed, was a regenerated threatre, different in purpose from both the commercial and court theatres.

During his time in Dresden, Wagner had read widely and intensively in classical literature. He was particularly moved by Aeschylus' *Oresteia*, which he found so overwhelming that it seems permanently to have distanced him from his own culture. After reading it, he claimed, "I lived in a condition of rapture from which I have never been able to reconcile myself entirely with modern literature. My ideas about the significance of drama and in particular about the theatre were decisively formed by these impressions." After reading Plato, he added, "I actually felt myself more at home in ancient Athens than in any conditions of modern life" (*ML*, II, 168). This discovery of ancient Attic culture allowed him to articulate with more clarity than before his objections to contemporary theatre and to develop a vision of the potential that theatre might achieve, which would serve as the basis for all his future theatrical undertakings.

Central to his discussion of theatre in "Art and Revolution" is an analysis of the Festival of Dionysus, which he described as the spiritual and cultural cynosure in the life of the people of ancient Athens. At the festival, performances of tragedy, centered around the great myths, led audiences to realize their national uniqueness and identity and to express "what was deepest and noblest in [their] consciousness" (*GSB*, X, 28). Through witnessing tragic performances, the Athenians became aware of both their common destiny as a people and the source of art lying within each individual's imagination. Performance in the theatre of Dionysus provided far more than mere entertainment or corrective morality. Rather, exploiting all the sensuous properties of human expression, it enabled individuals in the audience to experience themselves fully and freely, both as citizens and as natural beings. Theatre of this nature affirmed, articulated, and released vitalizing, sensuous impulses that allowed human beings to sense complementary harmonies within themselves and the world around them.[2]

Art is the highest activity of human beings who have developed their physical beauty in union with nature; the human being must find the

highest joy in the world of sense, if the tools of art are to be formed
from it; for the will to create artistically comes from the world of
sense alone. (*GSB*, X, 20)

Since this complete fulfillment of the senses had occurred only at the
Festival of Dionysus, for Wagner ancient Athens represented the single
point in history where artistic endeavor had been regarded as the ultimate
goal of individual and social striving. On the stage of its theatre, there was
no sense of dichotomy between the ideal form of expression toward which
art aspires and its actual achievement.

Wagner, who showed no awareness that performance in the theatre of
Dionysus might have been compromised by human imperfections, was
concerned mainly to use his idealized vision of the festival as a foil to
define all that was wrong with theatre in his own time. That theatre,
whether in France or Germany, he considered to be devoted solely to the
cause of commerce:

This is Art, as it now fills the entire civilized world! Its actual essence
is Industry; its moral purpose, money making; its aesthetic intention,
the entertainment of those who are bored. . . . Our modern theatrical
art materializes the ruling spirit of our public life . . . as no other art
can. . . . Just as Greek tragedy characterized the highest moment of
the Greek spirit, . . . [our theatre] is the bloom of decay, of an empty,
soulless, unnatural ordering of human affairs and relations. (*GSB*, X,
24–25)

While theatre in ancient Athens expressed the deepest consciousness of
the people, including their religious beliefs, theatre in modern Europe
deliberately avoided such expression and, in particular, was forced by
censorship and social convention to abjure any discussion or representation of religious matters. Thus, while the whole population of Athens
was expected to attend the Festival of Dionysus, modern European theatre
was only for the affluent classes, who expected nothing more than mind-
less entertainment in return for their patronage. In Athens, performers
engaged in theatre for the joy it instilled in them, while, in Europe,
performance was engaged in and judged a success only to the degree that
it led to financial reward for management, investors, and performers.
Indeed, the prime justification of modern theatre was its capacity to
provide employment. In short, theatre in Athens was an art, but in modern
Europe at best a handicraft.

While Wagner may have been uncritical in his judgment of classical theatre, he was aware that the conditions of modern life precluded even an approximate recreation of the Festival of Dionysus. Instead, it was the spirit of this theatre, rather than the details of its organization and manner of staging, that appealed to him. From the festival, he drew a vision of an art that opposed and refused to express the materialistic spirit of his own time. As it escaped from its slavery to commerce, such a theatre would finally achieve artistic maturity and become capable of teaching "the social impulse its noblest meaning and guide it toward its true direction" (*GSB*, X, 46). Such a statement indicates that in Wagner's post-revolutionary writings both the purpose and placement of theatre were fundamentally different from those implied in the Plan of 1848. In the earlier plan, Wagner had been content to see theatre as a means of cultivating the mores of citizens and thus, ultimately, as an agency adjunct to government and peripheral to central authority or, at least, dependent on it. Now, theatre itself became the central institution of society, its purpose being not just to educate citizens, but also to generate and perpetuate the vitality of the human race and to guide human society's perception of itself and under-standing of its goals. Through theatre, the "Folk," which Wagner defined as all those who feel "a collective want" (*GSB*, X, 55), could become conscious of their unity as a body of people.

This conception of theatre was a natural outgrowth of the revolutionary phase of Wagner's life, for through theatrical performances people would begin to understand purposes and patterns of life that were more compell-ing than the values propounded by traditional authority. This extreme radical thinking characterized only the earliest essay, "Art and Revolu-tion." In the later essays, the theatre maintained its function as the central institution of society, but the tone of the writing was more temperate and the exposition and analysis more systematic. For the theatre practitioner, the most useful of these later essays is perhaps the least known, "A Theatre for Zurich." In it, Wagner conducted his discussion with consistent atten-tion to the practicalities of theatre and, in so doing, provided a striking diagnosis of theatrical mediocrity, proposed a viable solution, and devel-oped further his own concept of theatre.

Wagner observed that while the people of Zurich regularly patronized their theatre, they seemed largely indifferent to it. He attributed this indifference to the inadequacy of the productions and performances. Most of the works seen in Zurich, whether operatic or spoken, were imports from Paris or the Italian opera houses, written for stages larger and more lavishly appointed than the one in Zurich. The expressive range and technical resources required by the central roles was beyond the power of Zurich performers, who lacked the experience and training of actors and singers in Paris. The affluent sector of the audience, having traveled to Paris or Italy, recognized the inadequacy of the performances, while the less affluent, who had not traveled, sensed it. Accordingly, performances failed to arouse the audience's enthusiasm, and this, in turn, demoralized the performers. The resulting event was little more than an expression of mutual contempt between audience and performers.

Wagner's solution to this state of affairs borrowed in part from his 1848 plan. It called for assembling a company of young people and training them in performance as thoroughly as other young people were trained in the sciences. Only after they had mastered the basics of acting would they learn to sing, and they would perform spoken drama in public before embarking on opera. Performances would only be given two or three times a week. While the proposal to provide formal training for performers was not novel (though no such facility actually existed at the time), Wagner's suggestion as to the material that they should perform was more innovative. The young performers should ignore the international repertoire and instead perform plays written specially for the company and the community by local writers, plays "sprung from those constantly present, deeply felt moods and relationships" of the community (GSB, IX, 169). In the context of German culture, a proposition such as this had aesthetic implications only suggested in the essay. The local plays produced would, no doubt, express the "inwardness" that Wagner considered distinctive about the German mentality, but such a quality was best articulated in lyrical form, not in the public mode of drama. Thus, the renewal of the theatre might well come from a small town like Zurich, since it would be more capable than larger cities of forming a theatre that expressed communal needs "entirely removed from all industrial concerns" (GSB, IX, 188). A new aesthetic of theatre might emerge as well. This was not a theme that Wagner chose to pursue in his essay, but it identified the major direction in which his own creative work was to lead.

In fact, the major purpose of Wagner's theoretical writings was not to present a complete theory of theatre but to explain to himself the new medium and form in which his next dramatic works would be cast. Characteristically, he described this transformation not as a purely personal phenomenon but as an event of epochal significance. The "total work of art," he claimed in "Art and Revolution," had disintegrated into the independent arts of dance, music, and poetry after a brief flowering in classical Athens. Right down to the present age, the history of the arts had been one of fragmentation. In their separate developments, the arts had betrayed their original function, which was to express the full joy of humanity in the consciousness of its existence. This betrayal was aggravated by the exploitation of the arts by the Christian church, which used them to articulate the slavish mentality it required of all believers. Subsequently, the arts were pressed into the service of autocratic European princes to proclaim an ideology of autocracy. In Wagner's own time, the arts served the needs of commerce. Modern opera, the most flagrant of commercial undertakings, sustained the separation of the arts by insisting on the primacy of music in all performances. To recombine the arts, Wagner claimed, would be a revolutionary undertaking, confuting their historical development over the past two-thousand years.

"The Art-Work of the Future" is a more measured essay than "Art and Revolution," no doubt because the residual fervor of the Dresden barricades was abating. Wagner described how the three "purely human" arts—dance (movement and gesture), tone (music), and poetry—could be combined so that each might find fulfillment in the other. When they are cultivated separately, he argued, each art can have no function beyond the display of technical accomplishment. Only in combination can each find its true purpose—music provides the dance with rhythms and melodies that give form and pattern to its movements and gestures, while poetry provides what Wagner called the shores that contain the potentially limitless realm of music. The visual art of architecture, painting, and sculpture can provide the physical environment for performance. This historic act of amalgamation was not totally without precedents, since Beethoven, Wagner claimed, had already experienced the limitations of pure music, which on its own can express only emotions without deeds or moral will. Beethoven's recourse to the words of Schiller's "Ode to Joy" (in the final movement of the Choral Symphony) initiated the process by which music could be liberated from its own restrictions.

The fallacies in Wagner's historical argument are many. After all, for generations, dance as ballet had utilized music as formative accompaniment; Beethoven's Choral Symphony did not represent the first time that words had been set to music, while purely orchestral and instrumental music continued to flourish after Beethoven. Furthermore, such dramatists as Shakespeare, Pedro Calderón de la Barca, and Goethe, all idolized by Wagner, had crafted their finest works without recourse to music. The historical argument was therefore insufficient to define the Total Work of Art. Wagner needed to arrive at a more specific definition to set the mark of individuality upon his own work and indeed to explain that future work to himself. This was the purpose of *Opera and Drama*.

At the very start of the book, Wagner stated succinctly what he considered to be the problem with modern opera, namely "a means of expression [music] has been made into the end, while the end of expression [the drama] has been made into a means" (*GSB*, IX, 21). The book was intended to describe how this situation could be remedied. He began by further surveys, first of the history of opera and then of drama. In these, he argued provocatively, though often with flagrant misrepresentations of the evidence, that the only proper stuff of drama is myth. Through myth we can discover the eternal interests of humanity. Myth reveals pure emotion devoid of temporal concerns and makes members of the audience aware of their existence on a plane of being beyond human time and physical space. The final section of the book is technical in the extreme as Wagner examined in the minutest detail how words and music could be combined to form one language. Central to his vision of opera, or "music drama" as he now called it, was the principle that no single element of performance should be subordinate to another element. Gluck, the eighteenth-century opera composer, had attempted a similar reform but, while Wagner acknowledged him as a forerunner, he argued that in fact Gluck subordinated music to the word, so that only the word carried the meaning of the dialogue and defined the action. Wagner wished to achieve an equality in which words, music, gestures, and scenery all could contribute to the total experience of the work. Equality between all elements and the seamlessness of their conjunction were crucial to Wagner's conception of the total work of art.

His theories might well have disappeared without trace, had it not been for the composition of the cycle *Der Ring des Nibelungen* (*The Ring of the Nibelung*) and the construction of the Festival Theatre at Bayreuth, the sole purpose of which was to provide a site suitable to stage the cycle. This combined project, upon which Wagner's fame both as a composer and as a man of the theatre substantially rests, is unique in the history of the theatre.

It would be difficult to overstate the vastness of Wagner's *Ring* cycle. It is one of the longest stage works ever written. The four music dramas, or "Festival Stage Plays" as Wagner finally called them, last approximately fifteen hours and can only be played on four separate evenings. Immensity alone is, of course, no guarantee of quality, but, for most theatregoers, the impact of the *Ring* is commensurate with its size. Accounting for both its historical importance and its effect in the theatre, the generally sober Ernest Newman referred to it quite simply as "one of the most stupendous dramas humanity has ever produced" (*NLRW*, II, 341–342), while Thomas Mann, restricting the time scale but broadening the generic scope, described it as "the most sublime, the most compelling work the [nineteenth] century has to offer."[3]

When he began work on the *Ring*, Wagner did not envision its performance in a conventional theatre; in fact, he wrote it as a deliberate attempt to tear himself from dependence on theatre as he then knew it. He intended both the conditions of performance and the manner in which the work was structured and composed to be radically different from whatever had come before. Early in the 1850s, in various letters and essays, he had outlined his conception of the proper theatre for the *Ring*, most notably in a letter to his old Paris friend, Ernst Benedikt Kietz, written in September 1850.

> Here where I am [Zurich] I would have a theatre built out of planks according to my design, have suitable singers come to me here, and set up everything necessary for this one special occasion, that I could be certain of a splendid performance of the opera. Then I would send out invitations everywhere, to all who are interested in my work, to make sure the auditorium is thoroughly occupied and—free of charge of course—give three performances one after another in a week, after which the theatre would be pulled down and the whole thing be at an end. (*SB*, III, 404–405)

Although Wagner modified his ideas as to how temporary the theatre should be (influenced, no doubt, by the single performance of works at the Festival of Dionysus), the basic ideas for the later Bayreuth Festival can be found here in embryo. Quite simply, the world was to come to *The Ring*; *The Ring* would not go to the world.

Decades were to pass before the building of the Bayreuth Festival Theatre and the completion of *The Ring*, for the composition of it occupied Wagner for much of the rest of his life. The idea for the cycle may have been suggested by the readings in German mythology that he undertook in connection with the composition of *Tannhäuser* and *Lohengrin*, although the old Germanic sagas and the story of the Nibelung race in particular had been posited as a subject for opera by critics in the 1840s. The first sign of his serious interest in the story was a scenario, "The Nibelungen Myth," completed in the summer of 1848, which outlined the plot of what would ultimately be *The Ring*, though important modifications were to follow. He initially intended to write a single opera, *Siegfrieds Tod* (*Siegfried's Death*), the poem for which he completed in November 1848. After this, he seems to have cooled to the project, and over the next two years, he drew up elaborate plans for stage works on Frederick Barbarossa, Jesus, and Wieland the Smith. He did not return to the Nibelung material until May 1851, when he was in the middle of writing *Opera and Drama*. This suggests that it was only then that this material finally struck him as particularly suited to the form of music drama that he was describing in his book.

Rereading *Siegfried's Death*, he realized that there was too much exposition, so he used much of the expository material as the basis for a "comedy" *Der junge Siegfried* (*Young Siegfried*) to precede the tragedy. The poem for this was completed in June 1851, but it contained too much exposition as well. Once again extracting the most essential expository material, Wagner proceeded to write the poems for two further works, *Das Rheingold* (*The Rhinegold*) and *Die Walküre* (*The Valkyrie*), which were completed by November 1852. The two Siegfried dramas were then revised in light of the preceding works and renamed *Siegfried* and *Götterdämmerung* (*Twilight of the Gods*). The whole was entitled *Der Ring des Nibelungen* (*The Ring of the Nibelung*), and Wagner first unveiled it to the public at four well-attended readings at the Hotel Bauer au Lac in Zurich between 16 and 19 February 1853. Fifty copies of the poem were published at his own expense.

The musical composition took vastly longer than the poems. For much of 1853, Wagner was depressed by his inability to set to work on the score. The blockage suddenly dissolved, he revealed, during a trip to Italy. Half asleep in an inn at La Spezia, he had the illusion of "sinking in swiftly flowing water" that resolved itself into "the chord of E flat major, which continually reechoed in broken form," which was to form the prelude to *The Rhinegold* (*ML*, II, 68). Although he was not to begin composition for another two months, the blockage had dissolved. The score of *Rhinegold* was completed in May 1854, and of *The Valkyrie* in March 1856, its composition having been delayed by a visit to London. The first two acts of *Siegfried* were completed in August 1857, but then Wagner stopped work on the cycle and did not resume sustained composition until the spring of 1869. The score of *Siegfried* was finally completed in February 1871 and that of *Twilight of the Gods* in November 1874. The first complete performance of the whole cycle took place in the Festival Theatre, Bayreuth, in August 1876, some twenty-eight years after the completion of the first scenario.

The Rhinegold is set in a prehuman time of dwarves, giants, and gods. Alberich, of the race of Nibelung dwarfs who labor within the earth, is sexually teased by the Rhine Daughters who guard a hoard of pure gold at the bottom of the river. In revenge, he steals the gold. As he does so, the Rhine Daughters tell him that whoever forges a ring from it and renounces the delights of love forever will gain all the wealth in the world.

Alberich makes such a ring and then sets the slavish Nibelung race to work amassing wealth for himself. He is, however, obstructed in his purpose by the god Wotan, who himself needs money in order to pay off two giants, Fafner and Fasolt, who have just built his great castle Valhalla. If they are not paid their due, they will possess Freia, the goddess whose golden apples keep the gods perpetually youthful. Wotan, accompanied by the fire-god Loge, descends into the earth, tricks Alberich out of his wealth, and wrests the ring from him, but not before Alberich curses it. In paying off the giants, Wotan wishes to keep the ring, but is forced to yield it to them to complete payment. As they are gathering up their wealth, the giants quarrel and Fafner kills Fasolt. The gods enter the fortress of Valhalla with Wotan deeply disturbed at the cost at which his power has been bought.

The Valkyrie takes place half in the world of humans, half in that of the gods. Two of Wotan's children by a human woman, Siegmund and Sieglinde, meet after years of separation. Siegmund has spent most of his life a miserable fugitive, while Sieglinde is bound in a loveless marriage to Hunding. They fall in love and flee from Hunding's house. High in the mountains, Wotan's wife, Fricka, demands that the two be punished for incest. Wotan, who had been protecting Siegmund in the hope that he would become the one being who might act with total free will, is forced to withdraw his protection. He orders his daughter, Brünnhilde the Valkyrie, not to prevent the death of Siegmund in the coming battle with Hunding, who is pursuing the lovers. Brünnhilde appears to the fleeing Siegmund and announces his coming death and elevation to Valhalla as a hero, but Siegmund refuses the apotheosis for he does not wish to be parted from Sieglinde. Brünnhilde, moved by the power of human love that his refusal demonstrates, promises to protect him. In the ensuing fight, however, Wotan's strength proves greater, and Siegmund is killed. Because she has disobeyed her father, Brünnhilde can no longer serve as one of the Valkyries, who bring the dead bodies of heroes to glory in Valhalla. Instead, she will be transformed into a mortal woman. After a moving parting, her father, much against his will, abandons her on a mountaintop, surrounded by a wall of fire that can be breached only by a man of indomitable will and strength. That man will be Siegfried, the still-to-be-born son of Siegmund and Sieglinde.

The "comedy" *Siegfried* takes place several years later. Sieglinde has died soon after giving birth to Siegfried, and the boy has been brought up in a cave by Mime, the brother of Alberich. Mime hopes that once his young charge has grown, he will be able to kill Fafner, the giant from *The Rhinegold*, who has transformed himself into a dragon and now guards

Alberich's wealth and the ring in a cave. Siegfried successfully forges the fragments of his father's sword into a new weapon and is led by Mime to the cave where Fafner sleeps, a journey that is watched by both Alberich and Siegfried's grandfather, Wotan. Siegfried kills the dragon and in so doing drinks its blood, which allows him to hear birdsong as language and to understand the true meaning behind people's words. Realizing that Mime wishes to kill him, he strikes Mime dead and then, directed by the song of a woodbird, seeks Brünnhilde on the mountain peak, carrying the ring with him. On the way up the mountain, he encounters Wotan in the guise of a traveler, defeats him in a brief fight and continues to the summit where he awakens Brünnhilde. The drama ends with the ecstatic union of Siegfried and Brünnhilde.

Twilight of the Gods dramatizes the death of Siegfried and the downfall of the gods. Siegfried, after consummating his union with Brünnhilde, leaves the ring in her possession and travels out into the world. At the hall of the Gibichungs, he meets Hagen, Alberich's son, who is plotting to regain the ring. Through the use of a love potion, Hagen makes Siegfried fall in love with the Gibichung princess Gutrune and persuades him, in disguise, to drag Brünnhilde from her mountain home so that she can marry Gutrune's brother Gunther. While assaulting Brünnhilde, Siegfried grabs the ring from her. Appalled at his seeming betrayal, Brünnhilde plots the death of Siegfried with Hagen and Gunther after her arrival among the Gibichung. Hagen eventually kills Siegfried in the course of a hunt, and his corpse is brought back to the Gibichung hall for cremation. As Hagen approaches Siegfried's body to tear the ring from its finger, however, the dead man's arm rises up to protect it. Brünnhilde then enters, having learnt that Siegfried was not knowingly unfaithful to her and immolates herself on the same funeral pyre as Siegfried. The flames ignite the Gibichung Hall and then Valhalla. After the conflagration, the Rhine overflows its banks, and the Rhine Daughters regain possession of the ring. The cycle ends, as it began, on a scene of elemental nature.

Given the extensive critical history of *The Ring*, it is impossible here to provide a comprehensive interpretation. The parameters of readings are normally considered to have been set, on the one hand, by George Bernard Shaw and Robert Donington. Shaw's critical essay *The Perfect Wagnerite* (1898) interprets the work as a quasi-socialist tract on the growth of capitalism. By contrast Donington, the musicologist who wrote *Wagner's Ring and Its Symbols* (1964), employs Jungian archetypal psychology to see the cycle as the realization of a single psychic consciousness. But as Deryck Cooke pointed out in his incomplete *I Saw the World End* (1979), a book that promised to be the most thorough analysis of *The Ring* ever undertaken, it is too multifaceted a work to be thrust into the procrustean bed of a single theory.

As Cooke exhaustively demonstrated, *The Ring* has little interest as a dramatization of ancient Germanic sagas and myths. While Wagner drew his material from this body of literature, in particular the *Volsunga Saga*, the *Poetic Edda, Thidriks Saga*, the *Nibelungenlied*, and the *Prose Edda, The Ring* is in essence a compression of various incidents from these sources and, without precedent, combines the Wotan and Siegfried myths, which were previously unassociated. Indeed, Wagner did not intend to revive the milieu of the sagas on stage but rather to create, through the saga material, a polemical allegory on the political, economic, and social life of his time.

Essentially Wagner saw three powerful, mutually antagonistic motive forces as fueling and forming that life. The first was the sheer lust for wealth and power, an ambition embodied by Alberich, deeply tempting to Wotan, and a potential goal for whoever possesses the ring. The second is the need for the ruler to govern and maintain power through treaties and contracts, a prerogative personified mainly in Wotan, whose discovery of the contradictions that destroy a ruler's authority provides the central tragic experience of the cycle. The third and most idealized force is the power of love, which Wagner hoped would transfigure a world distorted by the appetite for wealth and power; this force is exemplified first in the love of Siegmund and Sieglinde and then of Siegfried and Brünnhilde. The initial scenario and text of *Siegfried's Death* were informed by Wagner's enthusiasm for Ludwig Feuerbach. Feuerbach's optimistic philosophy held that belief in religious myth was but one phase in the evolution of humanity to complete freedom of will through reason and that love was one of the main intellectual stimuli to the revolution of 1848. Hence, in earlier drafts of the poem, the power of love triumphed unambiguously, and *Siegfried's Death* ended with Brünnhilde conducting Siegfried victoriously to Valhalla. In the course of composition, however, Wagner encountered the writings of Arthur Schopenhauer, whose philosophy of resignation deeply colored Wagner's pessimism, which grew during the early 1850s as a consequence of his personal setbacks and his sense of the defeat of progressive forces in the artistic and social world. Consequently, the revised ending of *The Ring*, while still realized in music that glorifies the redemptive power of love, is less utopian, for the power of wealth and political ambition have already effectively destroyed the durability of love.

The unforgettable impact of *The Ring* depends on many factors. For a start, it is as close as Wagner ever came to a dramaturgical masterpiece.

Between the long E flat minor chord that introduces *The Rhinegold* to the colossal spectacle closing *Twilight of the Gods*, one seems to have witnessed the history of the world from creation to doomsday. In actuality, the cycle dramatizes a less extended passage of time, namely the decline of the polytheistic pantheon of gods, who, in terms of contemporary allegory, might stand for the waning aristocracy of Central Europe. Nonetheless, even this is a mightily extended period for any drama to cover. Wagner does it most effectively by carefully selecting key incidents in the story and centering each of the four scenes of *Rhinegold* and each of the three acts of the other dramas around a single one. Accordingly, the action, far from being diffuse, is compressed and theatrically coherent. For example, in *The Valkyrie*, the climax of each act—Siegmund's removal of Wotan's sword from the roof-tree of Hunding's house in act 1, the fight between Siegmund and Hunding in act 2, and Wotan's passionate farewell to Brünnhilde that closes the work—is a moment that epitomizes the hour or so of previous action and clarifies the issues dramatized by that action. Furthermore, until *Twilight of the Gods*, there is no chorus and virtually no concerted singing; the action is conducted by a minimum number of characters. Thus, even though this drama, vast in scope, does not literally observe the unities of time and place, in actuality it is confined within rigorous limits reminiscent of the neoclassical drama. Moreover, while the settings of mountain peaks and forests and special effects (such as the dragon in *Siegfried*) challenge the imagination of the designer, *The Ring* does not, despite Wagner's ambitions, actually go beyond the conventional limits of the illusionistic stage. The settings can all be realized in the romantic-realistic style that was virtually universal in the production of opera in the mid-nineteenth century theatre. In contrast with the earlier *Flying Dutchman*, no attempt is made to exploit the physical setting as a metaphor for the inner life of any of the characters. Certain props, such as the ring, swords, and spears, have distinct meanings that relate to the thematic structure of the action, and certain settings (such as the citadel of Valhalla, glimpsed at the end of *The Rhinegold* and *Twilight of the Gods*) have symbolic meaning, but it is difficult to ascribe consistent metaphorical or thematic meanings to settings throughout *The Ring*. At base, a realistic aesthetic prevails.

Nevertheless, while the physical action is contained within the known limits of theatre and the sets function mainly just as settings, the music both materializes the action and projects it into realms of symbolic and unconscious experience in a way unprecedented in its time. Wagner had always insisted on the closest possible relationship between what was played in the orchestra and represented on stage. As he wrote in a letter of

1851, specifically about *Tannhäuser* but perhaps even more relevant to *The Ring*:

> My orchestral accompaniment never expresses anything for the ear which is not intended to be expressed on stage for the eye, be it through events on stage, through gestures, or only through facial expressions; where these are either absent or do not occur at precisely the corresponding passage in the orchestra, the understanding of my intentions is entirely impossible. (*SB*, IV, 122)

The complementarity of stage and orchestra is guaranteed by the flexibility of Wagner's media. The poems of his earlier operas were written in regular rhyming meter that encouraged the composition of broad melodies but was not always a suitable medium to articulate the fluctuating rhythms of the dramatic action or to explore character. The poem of *The Ring*, however, was written in *Stabreim*, an alliterative technique borrowed from the writers of the sagas. Since this verse is structured around the repetition of prominent consonants rather than the regular beats and rhyme of conventional poetry, Wagner could devise a musical language more sensitive to the demands of the changing action and more specific in the materialization of character, motive, and theme. It enabled him to adopt the leitmotif technique as the entire foundation of his musical structure. He could reduce the basic unit of music into phrases, even fragments a bar or two in length. Once the dramatic meaning of any leitmotif has been established, the earlier events with which it was associated will be recalled each time it is repeated. This becomes a notably complex process. Newman, for example, listed 198 leitmotifs in the entire *Ring*, while Donington found a mere 91.[4] It is difficult to identify all leitmotifs with certainty—Wagner actually discouraged the habit of labeling them—for they are subject to infinite variations in rhythm, orchestration, and key; one leitmotif will frequently be combined with another, often to form a third, thereby indicating a change in the dramatic action. An analysis of leitmotifs in all their various transformations can lead to a full understanding of the action. Their repetitions and variations invest that action with a clarity and compulsion not available either to the spoken drama or to opera as it had been practiced until that point. They recall and foreshadow events and underscore and focus audience attention on dramatic themes. Words and music carry the meaning of the work equally.

The huge orchestration is one of the most distinctive features of *The Ring*. As the structure of leitmotifs grows ever more complex, the prime function of the orchestra is to project the action into a symbolic realm that extends the audience's imagination beyond the limits of the stage. The orchestra also has the function of identifying the unconscious motivations of the characters and, like the chorus in classical drama, points to connections between individuals' actions and the larger symbolic framework. In this way, characters are experienced both as dramatic figures in their own right and as units in a larger pattern of events.

The leitmotif can also guide the audience's understanding of the action. As just one of countless possible examples, in *The Rhinegold*, Wotan's ambition to rule by contract is consistently indicated by a downward stepping tune in the lower strings. When this leitmotif is played by the brass, especially the trombones, it becomes powerful and oppressive, indicating Wotan's spear as a symbol of his actual rule by power, denying the freedom of the ruled. This leitmotif at times stands in opposition to another that indicates a contrary force. At the end of *The Rhinegold*, when Wotan is about to enter Valhalla, he realizes that his authority has been compromised and that his power will eventually pass. His gloom at this realization is dispelled as "he is seized by a grand thought." This thought, initially undefined, is represented by a gleaming, heroic phrase, played on the trumpet. Early in act 1 of *The Valkyrie*, this leitmotif is repeated frequently in association with a sword that Wotan once placed in the roof-tree of Hunding's hut on the occasion of the latter's wedding to Sieglinde. No one has since been able to remove it. As act 1 of *The Valkyrie* progresses, Siegmund and Sieglinde fall deeply in love, which is conveyed by some of Wagner's most poignant music. The music of their love intertwines with that of the sword until the two seem to be identical. Consequently, the sword becomes symbolic of the love that Wagner hoped would transform the human race. Siegmund's removal of the sword from the roof-tree indicates the consummation of that love and releases the hope that humanity will be made free by it. In act 2, as the action returns to the realm of the gods and Wotan realizes that Fricka's demands will force him to sacrifice Siegmund, the leitmotifs of the spear and the sword are heard in antithesis. The context augments the meaning of the sword leitmotif until it comes to express human free will, which is opposed to the necessary but repressive autocracy of the gods. In the climatic battle between Siegmund and Hunding at the end of act 2, Wotan's spear shatters Siegmund's sword and with it the hopes for humanity to determine its fate according to free will. At this moment, the two leitmotifs are heard in direct opposition to each other. Here words, music, action, and physical performance in unity realize the central thematic conflicts of *The Ring*. While the cycle does not challenge the physical limitations of the theatre, so close an interdependence of performance elements was unique in the nineteenth-century operatic theatre. Such coherence in realizing the full thematic implications of the action suggested a theatre of total integrity unprecedented in Wagner's time.

On 28 June 1857, Wagner wrote to Liszt:

> I have decided at last to give up my obstinate attempt to complete my *Nibelung*. I have led my young Siegfried into beautiful solitude in the forest; there I have left him under a linden tree and bidden farewell to him with heartfelt tears. . . . If I were to take up the work again, then this must either be made very easy for me, or I myself must be able to present it to the world as a gift in the fullest sense of the word. (*WLB*, II, 173)

His reasons for abandoning *The Ring* have been much debated. Although he endowed the action with dimensions that defied contemporary theatre, he was becoming increasingly discouraged by the lack of opportunity to have his most recent work performed. Because he insisted that *The Ring* should first be produced complete, he reduced even further the chances of hearing his music. There is distinct evidence too that, by 1857, his ideas on the interrelationship of words and music were changing and that he needed some time for his technique to mature before he could successfully complete the cycle. But perhaps the major reason for abandoning the work was that his interest in it, at least temporarily, was on the wane. While there is no decline in his musical inventiveness, the emotional temperature of the first two acts of *Siegfried* is distinctly lower and the dramatic momentum slacker than in the earlier works. In fact, circumstances in both Wagner's private and professional life suggested to him that the time was ripe for him to turn to new material. At this point, the story of Tristan and Isolde was better suited to express both his artistic and emotional needs.

NOTES

1. See Robert T. Laudon, *Sources of the Wagnerian Synthesis* (Munich: Katzbichler, 1979), for a full account of the origins of this theory.

2. For the vitalistic aspects of Wagner's theatre, see especially Michael Tanner, "The Total Work of Art," *The Wagner Companion*, ed. Peter Burbidge and Richard Sutton (New York: Cambridge University Press, 1979) (henceforward *TWC*).

3. Thomas Mann, "Der Ring des Nibelungen," in *Pro and Contra Wagner*, trans. Allan Blunder, ed. Patrick Carnegy (London: Faber and Faber, 1985), 192.

4. Ernest Newman, *The Wagner Operas* (New York: Knopf, 1949), 451–634; Robert Donington, *Wagner's Ring and Its Symbols* (London: Faber & Faber, 1963), 275–308.

Chapter 5

Romantic in Exile

Throughout the years in Paris and Dresden, the marriage of Richard and Minna Wagner had seemed fairly secure. In Dresden especially, Wagner's artistic success and the prestige of his position as Kapellmeister were enough to maintain domestic peace, even when his debts were mounting. Furthermore, the few letters from this time that Wagner wrote to Minna suggest that sexual attraction and a corresponding mutual sympathy were still very much alive. The flight to Zurich, however, precipitated a crisis. At first, Minna was unwilling to join her husband, who, she felt, had willfully destroyed his career in Dresden. Her refusal drew from Wagner a letter stating that the two of them might be fundamentally incompatible.

> What I have come to learn time and time again is that the *human being* is the most important thing in life, takes priority over everything else: but sadly for *you*, furniture and houses etc. often and habitually have more of a pull on your heart than the living human being.[1]

Eventually Minna joined him, but soon the first major crisis since the earliest days of their marriage occurred—the Laussot affair.

During his visit to France early in 1850, Wagner's feelings for Jessie Laussot, the wife of a Bordeaux wine merchant, grew so strong that he made plans to elope with her to Greece and the Orient. He was so confident of this scheme that he wrote to Minna requesting a separation, primarily on the grounds that she neither understood nor sympathized with his artistic vocation. There was, he claimed, a "fundamental difference in our natures" (*RWMWa*, I, 71). But the elopement was stalled by the intervention first of Jessie's mother and then of her husband, who forbade his wife to see Wagner. Wagner, after some embarrassing months spent in hotels around Lake Geneva, returned to Minna.

For some years after, all was outwardly calm in the Wagner marriage. Minna was a conscientious housewife, capable of making life comfortable on the relatively small sums of money from the Ritter pension, the scant royalties picked up from performances, the odd stipend for conducting, and contributions from various patrons. Nonetheless, her resentment at the perilous state of their finances grew. In return for the emotional stability she provided her husband, Minna required financial security—neither an unreasonable nor unusual bargain but one that Wagner was unable to honor. While his letters to Minna from this period show that he was intensely dependent on her, correspondence with his friends discloses that he was growing more alienated from her. Eventually, pity rather than love came to be the main bond tying him to her. Minna's health, moreover, was declining rapidly with the onset of the heart disease that would lead to her early death.

The immediate cause of the effective break-up of their marriage was Wagner's passion for Mathilde Wesendonk (Illustration 4), the wife of his most munificent patron. The Wesendonks had moved to Zurich from New York a year or two after the Wagners' arrival. Mathilde had been profoundly affected by the concerts of his music that Wagner had conducted in May 1853 and soon signs of a reciprocal attraction developed between the two. Relations between the families remained cordial enough for the Wesendonks to offer the Wagners a home in the gardens of their palatial new villa on a hill overlooking Zurich, the lake, and the Alps. Wagner believed that his idyllic retreat, the "Asyl" as he called it, would provide the perfect environment for the completion of his new music drama, *Tristan and Isolde*, which he had started the moment he had completed act 2 of *Siegfried*. In fact, when he and Minna moved in on 28 April 1857, they hoped that they had found a home for life.

All prospects of permanent residence were dispelled by the intensification of Wagner's passion for Mathilde. The proximity of their houses made intimate contact possible on an hourly basis, though it is unlikely that their love was consummated. Still, when Minna intercepted a letter from her husband to Mathilde containing an unambiguous expression of love, she not surprisingly considered that she had solid grounds for the outburst of jealousy that followed. This led to the eventual break-up of the household at the end of the summer of 1858, with Minna departing for Dresden and Wagner, still in exile from Germany,

Illustration 4. Mathilde Wesendonk, from a bust by Keiser. (Reproduced by permission of the Nationalarchiv der Richard-Wagner-Stiftung/Richard-Wagner-Gedenkstätte, Bayreuth.)

leaving for Venice. The Wesendonks remained in Zurich, facing the need to repair their seriously damaged marriage.

It was in the midst of the turmoil of his feelings for Mathilde that Wagner conceived and began work on *Tristan and Isolde*, an opera that contains some of the most overwhelming outpourings of romantic love to be found in any artistic medium. Mathilde and the idea of love she implanted in Wagner's mind were partially the inspiration, which dates back to the early days of their liaison. While Wagner was still working on *The Valkyrie*, he confided in Liszt:

> As I have never in my life enjoyed the actual happiness of love, I will create a monument to this most beautiful of all dreams, in which this love will be satisfied from the beginning to the end: I have drawn up in my head a *Tristan and Isolde*, the simplest but most full-blooded musical conception. (*WLB*, II, 46)

But however powerful Wagner's love for Mathilde—it took him several years to recover from the affair—she was not the sole reason for *Tristan*'s coming to light. While Wagner could be carried into the most abstruse realms of imaginative experience, he was also a practical man, and the practical man needed a theatre for his work. *The Ring* was still years from completion, and in its sheer length put it beyond the means of almost any opera house to produce. But, despite his avowed hatred of contemporary theatre, Wagner needed to see and hear his current work so that he could understand his progress as an artist, not to mention the money he might earn from royalties. He therefore intended *Tristan* to be a "thoroughly practicable work" (*WLB*, II, 175), with a comparatively small cast and modest scenic demands, putting it well within the capacity of even the smallest opera houses. In actuality, this putative repertory piece turned out, in the words of Ernest Newman, "to be the most difficult work in any dramatic genre which the world had yet seen" (*NWO*, 197).

This escalation in the difficulty of the work may reflect the influence of Schopenhauer upon Wagner's thought. Although *Die Welt als Wille und Vorstellung* (*The World as Will and Idea*) was first published in 1819, it was still virtually unknown when Wagner read it in 1854. The revelation it granted him was the single most important event in his intellectual development. For some years, the optimistic philosophy of Feuerbach that had informed the composition of his theory and the initial conception of *The Ring* had been wearing thin. His growing sense of isolation from the world and his fruitless passion for Mathilde undermined his earlier confidence. His discovery of Schopenhauer's philosophy, in which the height of human achievement is posited as "the final denial of the will to live" provided comfort, for it explained his own sufferings and gave them a philosophical dimension wider than his subjective experience. Indeed, the disclosure of the initial idea for *Tristan* to Liszt was prefaced by a declaration of the comfort that reading Schopenhauer had brought him:

> When I think back to the storms of my heart, to the terrible convulsion with which, against my will, it clung to the hope for life . . . I have now found a narcotic that finally helps me to sleep on wakeful nights; it is the heartfelt and inward longing for death: complete unconsciousness, total nonexistence, the disappearance of all dreams—unique, final redemption. (*WLB*, II, 45–46)

Though *The Ring* was capacious enough to absorb the Schopenhauerian view of the world in the figure of Wotan, Siegfried still manifested an earlier phase of Wagner's thought, so he needed material to express his new-found philosphical vision totally. This he found in the medieval legend of Tristan, which he had first encountered during his readings in Dresden but seriously considered as material for the stage only when the triple imperatives of practical, emotional, and intellectual needs combined to draw him away from *The Ring*.

Wagner's fervor for *Tristan* was apparent in his embarking on the poem immediately after completing act 2 of *Siegfried*. It took him a little more than a month to complete it, and, on 18 September 1857, he read the finished poem to a group of friends. In hindsight, this was a notable occasion, for the group included the three most important women in his whole emotional life—Minna, Mathilde, and Liszt's daughter Cosima, then married to Hans von Bülow but later to become Wagner's second wife. The proximity of Mathilde seems to have had a positive effect on his productivity, since by April 1858, the full score of act 1 had been completed and dispatched to the publishers for engraving. Progress on act 2, however, was inhibited by his marital crisis, and Wagner could complete it only after he had settled in Venice in the fall of 1858. He chose this city because the absence of modern urban traffic and the atmosphere of beauty and decay in a dreamy setting where the sea seemed to mingle with the sky struck him as a manifestation of Schopenhauer's renunciation of the will to live. His diary, written in the form of unsent letters to Mathilde, is filled with idyllic descriptions that mingle the landscape and his longing for her. His sojourn in Venice allowed him both to objectify his love for Mathilde and to compose the great love scene of act 2, in which the height of erotic fulfillment is felt by the lovers as an experience akin to death, as a renunciation of the world. But Wagner could not complete *Tristan* in Venice. In March 1859, the Venetian authorities insisted that he leave, due to an expulsion order from the ruling Austrians who had an intense suspicion of Wagner's revolutionary past. He then moved to Lucerne, eventually finishing the opera there on 6 August 1859.

While *The Ring* was the central, certainly the most gigantic, achievement of Wagner's career, *Tristan* might be considered as historically the more important work. Musicologists consider it a pivotal composition of the nineteenth century, for in it Wagner began to dissolve the tonal structure that for centuries had determined the basic structure of classical orchestral and vocal music, thereby initiating modern atonalism. The chord that opens the opera is only resolved four hours later when Isolde expires over Tristan's body—an exercise in musical suspense that intensely materializes the yearning for union in death, which is the lovers' goal. *Tristan* is equally important in the history of the theatre, for in theme, dramaturgy, and stage technique, it prefigures both the symbolist theatre of the late nineteenth century and the minimalist tendencies of the twentieth. Perhaps it is not irrelevant that, while engaged in its composition, Wagner was more removed from contact with the practical theatre than at any other time in his life. Despite his ambition to write a stageworthy opera, *Tristan* is in spirit the most removed from the standard practices of the nineteenth-century theatre of all his works.

Wagner compressed his medieval sources, principally Gottfried von Strassburg's epic *Tristan*, into three acts, each of which, like the acts of *The Ring*, culminates in a single climactic event. In act 1, Tristan is escorting Isolde, an Irish princess, to Cornwall where she is to marry his master King Marke. Isolde is obsessed with Tristan, ostensibly because he killed her betrothed Morold in battle, but in truth because she is deeply in love with him. She persuades him to drink a poisoned draught with her, but her confidante Brangaene substitutes a love potion, and the two admit their ardent love as the boat on which they are sailing arrives in Cornwall. In act 2, the lovers meet while Marke and his court are hunting, but their rapturous love-making is interrupted by the return of the king, who has been informed of the lovers' betrayal of his honor by Tristan's "friend," Melot. The act closes as Tristan is wounded in a fight with Melot. In act 3, Tristan, delirious from his wound, has been conveyed to Kareol, his castle in Brittany. Here he feverishly expresses his yearning for Isolde who eventually arrives to tend his wounds. He dies in her arms. Marke arrives to forgive the lovers, but Isolde, in throes of passion, expires over Tristan's dead body.

Almost all the characteristic features of conventional nineteenth-century dramaturgy are avoided in this work. The theatrical taste of the time was for densely plotted stories and abundant action (certainly features of *The Ring*), but, in *Tristan*, physical action is reduced to a minimum. Incidents that further the plot are included only when absolutely necessary, and exposition is so cursory that incidental figures such as Melot are incompletely incorporated into the action. Most expository passages, like Isolde's narration in act 1 and Tristan's recalling of the past during his fever in act 3, are of interest not because of what they explicitly narrate but for what they reveal of the narrator's present state of mind. The opera is devoted so exclusively to incarnating the emotions of the lovers that the brief flurries of action concluding each act are painfully obtrusive. But that pain does not last for long, since Wagner did not construct his plot on the traditional basis of dramatic action—conflict. King Marke, the most obvious antagonist, is in fact a highly sympathetic character. The sorrow he expresses in his moving soliloquy after discovering Tristan and Isolde together deepens rather than lessens his love for them, thus drawing the audience even more closely into the world of the drama. Unity rather than division is the essential experience of *Tristan and Isolde*.

If this defusion of conflict prefigures the early modernist drama at the end of the nineteenth century, in particular the later plays of Ibsen and the symbolism of Strindberg and Maurice Maeterlinck, so too does the use of the set. Wagner here returned to the principle of scenery as expressive of the inner life of the character, as in *The Flying Dutchman*, although he extended it symbolically to encompass broader realms of the lovers' passion for each other, which they articulate as an experience closer in spirit to death than to life. In the course of act 1, the heavy curtains that separate Isolde's quarters from the deck of the ship serve as a spatial metaphor for the division between the harsh public world of politics and warfare and the nurturing realm of romantic love. In act 2, this dichotomy is made explicit through the contrast of light and dark, light standing for quotidian reality and darkness for the power of eros through which the two lovers discover the deepest truths about themselves. Tristan's desolate castle in act 3 and the tormenting, blinding light in which it is bathed articulates the disorder created by his yearning for Isolde. In actuality, it was beyond the conceptual and technical capacity of nineteenth-century scenographers to realize this metaphorical potential, but, in the modern theatre, *Tristan and Isolde* has been instrumental in bringing about important changes in the scenographic sensitivity of designers.

The opera has, of course, survived also for its score, unique in Wagner's output for its sheer beauty and opulence. This he realized as he composed it, writing in his diary:

> What music it is becoming! I could work my whole life at this music alone. O, it grows deep and beautiful, and the sublimest marvels adapt so smoothly to its sense; I have never created anything like this! I dissolve in this music.[2]

Dissolution is an appropriate image. The music of *Tristan* has none of the clear outline and specificity of *The Ring*. Only rarely are its leitmotifs pictorial, descriptive, or representative; they elude definition, indefinability being their essence. Wagner described this music as "the profound art of resonant silence" (*RWMWe*, 68). It materializes experiences centered around the nexus of erotic love and death that lie beyond the capacity of words to describe.

In *The Ring*, music amplifies meanings within the words, so words and music have equivalent status in accordance with the theory of the total work of art. In *Tristan*, words are not so important. There is less alliteration, more assonance and, in the love scene of act 2 especially, frequent rhymes, all of which have the effect of blending the words into the music through the vowels. The seamless union of the separate arts, an essential feature of Wagner's theory, is maintained, but music is now the preeminent unifying language. In the passages where Wagner retreated most from the word, he abandoned the rule so rigorously practiced in *The Ring* that, in the cause of verisimilitude, no two characters should sing together. In the love scene especially, the voices of Tristan and Isolde, carried on swelling waves of sound, intertwine as a sign of their total oneness, of both having lost their identity in each other. Like the stage settings, the musical dialogue does not reflect everyday reality but is a metaphor for emotional experience.

As modern critics have pointed out,[3] Wagner did not entirely abandon the balance of words and music. In Tristan's soliloquy in act 3, for example, words regain an equal presence, sometimes as narrative, when he recalls his childhood, and other times as an expression of his yearning for Isolde. In this passage, the graphic quality of the music captures viscerally a mind on the brink of insanity. Wagner's music, overwhelming in its depiction of erotic passion, is also attuned to depicting the dynamics of the conscious and unconscious mind. At this point, Wagnerian music drama borders on modern psychological drama.

With *Tristan and Isolde*, Wagner had extended the musical and scenic parameters of the operatic stage beyond contemporary conceptions of what was possible. It was not surprising, therefore, that he wished to see it staged, but no less surprising that he could find no one willing to stage it. Initial plans were made for a production at Karlsruhe, but these were abandoned because of technical problems and tensions between Wagner and the theatre's intendant Eduard Devrient, the historian of acting and an erstwhile colleague back in the Dresden years. The only city that might have had a theatre with the technical equipment and artistic personnel that Wagner required was Paris, so he decided, once again, to seek his fortune in the French capital. Consequently, he moved there from Lucerne in September 1859.

Despite Minna's continuing fury at Wagner's affair with Mathilde, which she insisted was still in progress, husband and wife decided to give their marriage one more try. Minna arrived in Paris in November to take charge of a small though pleasant house that Wagner had rented near the Champs Elysées, but harmony was never restored. The state of Minna's health prevented any sexual relations, a condition to which Wagner may not have been entirely averse, so the old intimacy and confidence were lacking. The move to Paris also initiated a series of financial crises that increased in size and urgency until 1864 when Wagner, by then living in Vienna, was once more on the verge of being arrested for debt. During this period, funds were not lacking; he actually managed to extract larger sums from royalties than before and increasingly munificent contributions from those patrons rash enough to back him in the hope of some return on their investment. Nonetheless, his extravagant mode of living and the risky artistic enterprises of this period drained his resources until he was quite literally penniless.

Soon after his arrival in Paris, he tried to arrange a season of his works in the spring season after the Italian Opera had closed. He intended to stage *Tannhäuser*, *Lohengrin*, and finally *Tristan* in model performances to be given by the best available German singers. Not surprisingly, the project fell through, due to lack of funding and the unwillingness of German theatres to release their best singers before the end of their seasons. In order to raise money and introduce his music to the Parisians, Wagner arranged three concerts that he conducted early in 1860. Here he again encountered a situation familiar from earlier days in Dresden, namely, that his music was a popular success while the press was almost universally hostile. Wagner ungenerously attributed this to the influence of Meyerbeer, still the most powerful composer in Paris and considered by Wagner to be his mortal enemy. Nevertheless, less conservative figures such as Berlioz were also lukewarm in their reception of his music, since it challenged conventional expectations of extended and developed melody as the core of musical structure. Two concerts that he gave in Brussels were similarly received. In all cases, the box-office receipts were less than expenses, so Wagner was unable to reap any profit to float his operatic projects.

At last, his fortunes appeared to improve. In March 1860, the Emperor Napoleon III ordered *Tannhäuser* to be given at the Paris Opéra. Nothing, he decreed, should be allowed to hinder Wagner from achieving a production that he considered perfect. Auguries for the success of the project were not, however, favorable. For a start, political rather than artistic considerations had determined the Emperor's decision, the production having been ordered at the urging of Princess Metternich, the wife of the Austrian ambassador, who had befriended Wagner. Moreover, while the Opéra would do all it could to aid Wagner, it was clear that the customs of the house would not be changed to suit him. In particular, it was *de rigeur* that each opera should include a ballet in act 2, so that members of the Jockey Club who wished to see their mistresses dancing would not have to finish their dinners early to do so. Wagner, informed of this custom, was not entirely unaccommodating. He allowed it to suggest to him an orgiastic ballet that would link the overture to the first scene in Venus' cave, thereby bridging an awkward transition in the original, Dresden version of the opera, but he adamantly refused to place the ballet in the middle of act 2, since it would make no artistic sense there. From this position he would not budge. In fact, the ballet, composed in the chromatic manner of *Tristan*, is stylistically incongruous with the rest of the opera, but since it gives Venus and the forces of sensuality from which Tannhäuser struggles to free himself greater dramatic presence, the conflict at the heart of the opera is accordingly intensified.

Preparation for the production was extraordinary; over 164 rehearsals were held. Wagner had the run of the Opéra and was mightily impressed by its technical apparatus and its process of production, which combined, he observed laconically, "highest dullness and extraordinary precision" (*ML*, III, 237). Nevertheless, disaster seemed unavoidable. First, Wagner suffered a severe bout of meningitis in November 1860, which drained his energy; his absence, in turn, sapped the enthusiasm of the company. After his return, when rehearsals began to improve, the tenor Albert Niemann, hired from Hanover for a whole year solely to sing Tannhäuser, was intimidated by rumors of public and press hostility to the production and refused to cooperate with Wagner. Worst of all, the rules of the Opéra dictated that only the resident conductor could lead the performance. In this case, the conductor was Pierre-Louis Dietsch, the man who twenty years earlier had composed the failed *Vaisseau fantôme*, based on the scenario for *The Flying Dutchman*. A musician of limited comprehension, he was incapable of giving the complex score any form or coherence. All in all, despite the technical superiority of the Opéra, Wagner's suspicions of the inadequacy of the contemporary theatre, even in Paris, the fount of all that was modern and fashionable, were only too well confirmed.

Tannhäuser was eventually given three performances on 13, 18, and 24 March 1861, the occasion being among the most spectacular fiascoes in opera history. While the performance was far from perfect, the decisive factor in the production's failure was the conduct of the Jockey Club. Most accounts suggest that, had these gentlemen not been present in the auditorium, the work might ultimately have been a popular success; indeed, Wagner even considered the first night to be far from a disaster. But the whistling, catcalls, and heckling of the Jockey Club created havoc in the auditorium and disrupted all concentration. Although Wagner's refusal to write a ballet for act 2 has traditionally been considered the reason for their hostility, more compelling was their dislike of Princess Metternich and of German influence in the French court. Wagner too was politically suspect, for, despite the Emperor's patronage, he still had not lived down his reputation as a revolutionary and was therefore hardly a man to appeal to the conservatives of the Jockey Club. The failure of *Tannhäuser* at the Paris Opéra was inevitable.

Despite or perhaps because of the furor, advanced box-office sales for *Tannhäuser* were extremely heavy, so the administration wished to keep it in the repertoire. But Wagner insisted on withdrawing his score, principally, he claimed, because, once audiences quieted down, they would quickly become aware of the artistic inadequacies of the performance (*GSB*, II, 120–121). As a result, he denied himself any profit from over a year's work on the production. Ultimately, his total payment from the Opéra was 750 francs, whereas the recalcitrant tenor Niemann was paid 54,000 francs. Given such vast disparities, Wagner's financial troubles cannot be considered to be entirely his fault, and his resentment at the power of the virtuoso performer appears to have had valid personal grounds.

His immediate concern after the *Tannhäuser* production was to find a theatre capable of staging *Tristan*. Fortunately, the previous summer he had been granted a partial amnesty by the King of Saxony, which allowed him to travel in all German states except Saxony. The possibility of a production at Karlsruhe was still open, so, with the encouragement of the theatre's patron, the Grand Duke of Baden, Wagner traveled to Vienna to recruit singers. It was in Vienna that he first heard *Lohengrin* in an outstanding performance, which ended with his rapturous reception by the audience. So impressed was he by the quality of the Vienna company and the sympathy of the audience that he eagerly agreed to a suggestion by the Court Opera management that Vienna rather than Karlsruhe should stage the première of *Tristan*. Subsequent dealings with the opera house proved cruelly disappointing. *Tristan* was given 77 rehearsals between October 1861 and May 1863 but was eventually abandoned as unperformable. The chief hindrance was the tenor, Alois Ander, who suffered from crippling bouts of hoarseness that were psychosomatic in origin. As rehearsals progressed, further difficulties and tensions developed, especially between Wagner and Luise Dustmann, his Isolde, leading to the ultimate demise of the project.

Although Vienna remained his headquarters during this period, Wagner traveled restlessly in search of a home where he could have peace to compose and a patron to provide him with financial security. He would find neither. Minna and he had separated when they closed down their Paris household. Only after several months of traveling between Vienna and Paris, which included an unsuccessful visit with the Wesendonks in Venice, did Wagner find a temporary pied-à-terre in Biebrich, a village on the banks of the Rhine, close to Wiesbaden. He chose this spot for its beauty and its proximity to Mainz, where the publishing house of Schott was located; the owner, Franz Schott, had agreed to support Wagner while he was writing his next opera, *The Mastersingers of Nuremberg*. Soon after settling there in February 1862, Minna paid him a brief visit, but her stay was so wracked by quarrels and accusations that Wagner could only describe it as "ten days of hell."[4] The following spring and summer were surprisingly rejuvenating. A long visit from the Bülows led to closer intimacy between Wagner and Cosima. The noted tenor Ludwig Schnorr von Carolsfeld and his wife Malvina also spent time in Biebrich, while Wagner developed the warmest of friendships with a local woman, Mathilde Maier, and enjoyed an affair with Fredericke Meyer, a leading actress in the nearby Frankfurt theatre. It was a summer of Bohemian living, which shocked the bourgeoisie of Biebrich, but it was a tonic for Wagner's frayed nerves.

Of course, none of this improved his finances, and, when Schott withdrew his patronage because progress on *The Mastersingers* was so slow, Wagner was forced to search for other means to support himself. Conducting was most readily to hand. From September 1862 through to the end of 1863, he accepted several invitations to conduct throughout

Central and Eastern Europe. He began with *Lohengrin* at the Frankfurt opera and later, after the ban on travel to Saxony was rescinded, conducted at Leipzig. From there, he traveled to Dresden, where he spent four days with Minna, the last time they were to see each other. He went on to Vienna, where he gave three concerts in the Theatre an der Wien; these were a popular success but, as usual, a financial disaster. After visiting Prague, he traveled to Russia, where five concerts in St. Petersburg and three in Moscow turned out, for once, to be exceptionally profitable. Flush with money, he returned to Vienna, where he rented a pleasant house in the suburb of Penzing; this he fitted out with the most extravagant luxury, almost at once running through his Russian profits. Further concerts in Pest, Prague, and various German cities followed. He returned to Vienna in December 1863 to celebrate Christmas in a characteristically excessive manner, bestowing expensive gifts on friends and servants alike. The combined costs of his household expenses and his generosity vastly overstretched his budget. By March 1864, with creditors at his door, he was forced to flee Vienna to avoid arrest.

At no other time in his life does Wagner appear to have been quite as helpless and as desperate as at this point. Despite his exuberant behavior, letters indicate that he felt totally isolated from a world that showed little interest in him. In particular, he was distressed by his continuing failure to find any theatre to perform his latest works. This so discouraged him that even he lost his desire to compose. He had made no progress on *The Mastersingers* since Biebrich. All that the public knew of his work since 1850 were extracts given in concerts. The total artistic vision, the effect of the work as theatre as well as music, was something that no one, not even Wagner himself, could appreciate and understand.

He left Vienna in need of a haven. This was not to be found with the Wesendonks. Although they had kept in contact and had even occasionally invited him to their house, his demands on Otto's bank account and their marriage, which had survived the crisis of 1859, were exorbitant. They were willing to pay him a small allowance but only if he stayed away. Wagner found temporary asylum with an old friend, Eliza Wille, who lived in Mariafeld, close to Zurich. Here, depressed, listless, and convinced that he had no future, Wagner felt totally abandoned. Only a miracle could save him. "*A light* must show itself," he wrote to the composer Peter Cornelius. "*Some person* must appear and give me his energetic help *now*" (*RWFZ*, 372). That someone was not to be Eliza Wille's husband François, who, discovering Wagner at his house on his return from a business trip, insisted that he vacate the premises at once. Wagner left Mariafeld on 29 April 1864 and traveled to Stuttgart in the vague hope that the Kapellmeister there, Karl Eckert, might be able to produce one of his operas. While staying in Stuttgart, the savior he was looking for suddenly appeared.

NOTES

1. *Richard Wagner an Minna Wagner*, 2 vols. (Berlin: Schuster & Loeffler, 1908), I, 53 (henceforward *RWMWa*).

2. *Richard Wagner an Mathilde Wesendonk: Tagebuchblätter und Briefe, 1853–1871* (Berlin: Duncker, 1904), 83 (henceforward *RWMW*).

3. Jack Stein, *Richard Wagner and the Synthesis of the Arts* (Detroit: Wayne State University Press, 1960), 135–143 (henceforward *RWSA*).

4. *Richard Wagner an Freunde und Zeitgenossen*, ed. Erich Kloss (Berlin: Schuster & Loeffler, 1909), 300 (henceforward *RWFZ*).

Chapter 6

The King's Friend

In April 1863, Wagner published the complete poem of the *Ring*-cycle, prefaced by an essay describing the ideal festival theatre in which he hoped the work would first be performed. Since such an institution had no chance of surviving in a commercial environment, he called for a German prince to serve as patron to the cause. "Will this Prince be found?" was the concluding question of the preface (*GSB*, II, 132). This work was read by Crown-Prince Ludwig of Bavaria (Illustration 5), an idealistic, melancholy, and lonely young man, who, having read *Opera and Drama* at the age of twelve and seen *Lohengrin* at fifteen, had become the most fervent of Wagnerians. Ludwig was not especially musical, but he was inflamed by Wagner's vision of art as the salvation of the human race, which was being destroyed by its obsession with material gain. On 10 March 1864, when Ludwig was only eighteen, he ascended the throne of Bavaria. One of his first acts as king was to declare that he would be the royal patron whom Wagner was seeking. He therefore dispatched his Cabinet Secretary, Franz von Pfistermeister, to find the composer. Pfistermeister arrived in Vienna, only to discover that Wagner had taken flight from his creditors, so he followed the trail through Zurich to Stuttgart. On finding Wagner there, he issued him an instant summons to an audience with Ludwig.

The audience, which took place in Munich early in May 1864, left both men steeped in profound admiration, even adoration, for each other. Wagner offered Ludwig an artistic realm that seemed to realize tangibly his most incorporeal and mystical longings, while Ludwig provided Wagner

Illustration 5. King Ludwig II of Bavaria, 1865. (Reproduced by permission of the Nationalarchiv der Richard-Wagner-Stiftung/Richard-Wagner-Gedenkstätte, Bayreuth.)

with unquestioning worship, complete understanding, the opportunity to have his works performed at the Munich Court Theatre, and freedom from financial woes. Ludwig offered to pay off all Wagner's debts, give him free accommodations, and provide him with a generous stipend. Wagner wrote to Mathilde Maier:

He shows the deepest understanding of my nature & of my need. He offers me everything that I need to live, to create, and to perform my works. I am to be his friend, nothing more: no appointment, no functions to fulfill. It is all I ever wished for.[1]

The advent of Ludwig at what had seemed the nadir of his career must have struck Wagner as little short of miraculous.

He traveled at once to Vienna to pay off his debts and then returned to spend the summer at Lake Starnberg outside Munich where Ludwig housed him in a villa close to one of his castles. Here a second significant and ultimately beneficial change occurred in Wagner's circumstances, when Cosima, the wife of Hans von Bülow, Wagner's most devoted and talented acolyte, arrived to stay with her children. For years, the Bülow marriage had been unhappy; in fact, Cosima may once have been on the brink of suicide. During the summer at Biebrich and in November 1863, when Wagner had visited the couple in Berlin, a powerful attraction had grown between her and the composer. The relationship was consummated soon after Cosima's arrival in Bavaria. Later she was joined by her husband who had probably been told of the change in his marital situation. Since Minna was still alive and Wagner would not contemplate divorce, a secret *ménage à trois* was the only arrangement possible. From this point on, Wagner and Cosima remained devoted to each other.

In the autumn, Wagner moved to Munich, where he was put up, rent-free, in a splendid house on Briennerstrasse, close to the Royal Palace and its theatres. At the expense of the king, he decorated and furnished the house in his customarily lavish manner. By now, the Bülows were indispensable to him, Cosima for emotional reasons and Hans because he was the only conductor capable of understanding Wagner's music and eliciting from an orchestra acceptable performances of it. Furthermore, Wagner's initial plans for Munich included not only a festival theatre but also the establishment of a music school in which to train students in dramatic performance, both sung and spoken. Bülow would be a founding member of this school. Other disciples, such as the composer Peter Cornelius, were later summoned to Munich as well to help in the enterprise. Meanwhile, Cosima's devotion to Wagner increased. She spent most of her time at his house, making herself indispensable as his secretary, a relationship that quickly aroused the curiosity of Munich society.

Wagner's preeminent concern was to arrange the first performance of *Tristan and Isolde*. After this, he planned model performances of all his major works, to be followed by a production of the completed *Ring*-cycle and other still-unwritten music dramas. These would be staged in a specially built festival theatre where the quality of performance would not be marred by the routine that Wagner insisted was characteristic of all German theatres. The theatre would be designed by Gottfried Semper on a commission from Ludwig. The first step toward this goal was a model production of *The Flying Dutchman*, until then not seen in Munich. Wagner himself conducted the first performance on 4 December 1864, and the enthusiastic reception demonstrated that his honeymoon with Ludwig and the Bavarian social and political establishment was not yet over. Even critics normally hostile to Wagner received the work warmly, recognizing the spinning chorus and love duet of act 2 as major steps in the progress toward a new mode of music drama. The picturesque sets by Anton II Quaglio and Heinrich Döll were striking, the stage production less so. Nevertheless, the quality of both the musical performance and stage technology was sufficient to convince Wagner that, if he were allowed to import his own soloists, Munich would provide a suitable venue for the first performance of *Tristan and Isolde*.

The most crucial of these imports were the tenor Ludwig Schnorr von Carolsfeld and his wife Malvina, who were to sing the title roles. Along with Schröder-Devrient, Schnorr fulfilled Wagner's concept of the ideal performing artist. Despite his exceptional corpulence, his understanding and complete sympathy with Wagner's complex characters made him an ideal interpreter. In fact, Wagner claimed that through Schnorr he came to understand his own creative process more clearly. He was, Wagner claimed, as powerful an actor as Edmund Kean or Ludwig Devrient (he had seen the latter), while his singing was so ample that "the orchestra disappeared completely in the presence of the singer, or—more correctly— seemed to be preserved in his performance" (*GSB*, II, 153).

The rehearsals for *Tristan*, which began on 10 March 1865, were an unusually happy time for Wagner, since for once he was working with artists he could respect in a theatre that offered few shortcomings in terms of stage presentation. Wagner devoted his energies to staging, while Bülow confined his efforts to the orchestra. In the process of rehearsal, Wagner became aware of *Tristan*'s uncommon intimacy. In the baroque Residenztheater, where the first rehearsals took place, the music sounded "not strong, but uncommonly clear and light," while the proximity of the audience to the stage was ideal for a work in which "everything touches on the representation of the purely human. The incidents are of a thoroughly internal, delicate kind; here a quiver in the face, a blink of the eyes is telling."[2] In contrast with his other works, *Tristan* seemed a chamber opera whose impact would be lost in the broader expanses of the Court Theatre. Nevertheless, the king insisted that the production move to this less hospitable space, a move to which Wagner unwillingly acceded, though even he ultimately acknowledged its necessity, admitting that his oversized orchestra swamped the singers in a small theatre. Crucially, his experience of the Residenztheater intensified his ambition for a theatre of his own, in which the intimacy of the drama and the immensity of the music could be reconciled.

By the time of the first production of *Tristan*, Wagner's honeymoon with Munich was over. His extravagance and irregular relationship with Cosima made him a controversial figure, and his reputation was not helped by Bülow, who, though a brilliant conductor, was an irascible individual. Once during rehearsals, Bülow was understood to refer to Munich audiences as *Schweinehunde* (pig-dogs), giving rise to a press outcry that nearly closed down the production. The potentially hostile public climate strengthened the acute discomfort Wagner anticipated feeling when the work was first performed. He therefore invited an audience of his "friends" from near and far to guarantee a sympathetic reception for *Tristan*. Even so, on the day set for the first performance, 15 May 1865, he was unable to fill the entire auditorium with partisans. Still, a measure of the international interest in his work could be taken from the hundreds of people who came from all over Europe to be present at the première.

The day turned out to be among the most disappointing of his life. It started with bailiffs who, on behalf of a still-unpaid creditor from years back, served an order of distraint on his possessions in Briennerstrasse. No sooner had Wagner met this crisis, by persuading the Royal Treasury to bail him out, than news arrived that Malvina Schnorr had gone hoarse while taking a steambath. Consequently, the performance had to be postponed, and the reputation that the work had already acquired as being dangerous to singers' voices was, not surprisingly, reinforced. The Schnorrs, meanwhile, retired to a local spa to await Malvina's recovery.

The first performance eventually took place on 10 June 1865. Wagner considered it to be a model, musically, mimetically, and from the point of view of staging. Quaglio and Döll's sets were suitably atmospheric in the romantic-realistic mode of the time (Illustration 6), while the performers held the audience spellbound. Although they found the lack of action and the dissolving tonality of the score unfamiliar, even unnerving, the recep-

Illustration 6. Closing scene of act 1 of *Tristan and Isolde*, Munich, 1865. (From a sketch by Theodor Pixis. Reproduced by permission of the Nationalarchiv der Richard-Wagner-Stiftung/Richard-Wagner-Gedenkstätte, Bayreuth.)

tion was warm, with the exception of occasional hissing at the end of the acts. The Schnorrs in particular were applauded whenever they took their bows. Critical reception was mixed, ranging from the ecstatic to the vicious. Röckel, Wagner's companion during the Dresden revolution, referred to *Tristan* quite simply as "the most beautiful and noble work [of art] the world yet possesses." At the other extreme, the correspondent for the *Augsburger Postzeitung* considered it little better than "unbroken howling. . . . The orchestra outdid itself in eccentricities, disharmonies, disconnected, chaotic phrases, blustering uproar."[3] Such dichotomies in opinion were common, serving to widen the gap between Wagner and the conservative mainstream.

The dangers that Wagner's music posed to whoever was rash enough to sing it seemed to be confirmed a mere three weeks after the last performance. Ludwig Schnorr died, possibly as a result of a chill caught during the long passages in act 3 when he lay on stage in a draught that no one had done anything to block. Only twenty-nine years old, his death was a severe blow to Wagner, who had envisioned him as a major participant in his future plans for a model theatre and school and as the ideal interpreter of his roles.

While the production of *Tristan* elevated Wagner's artistic reputation in Munich, it did little to allay public fears over his influence on the king. At this time, the independence of Bavaria was severely threatened by the rivalry between Austria and Prussia to become the dominant power in the emerging united Germany. To withstand the aggressive policies of Otto von Bismarck, Bavaria needed a powerful figurehead for its monarch, a role to which Ludwig was entirely unsuited. While he was a man of shrewd judgment, he had a profound distaste for politics and a pathological dislike of public appearances. Instead, he wished to immerse himself in entranced contemplation of the beautiful, whether in music, poetry, or architecture. Wagner's friendship intensified the king's penchant toward introspection, which in turn weakened the stability of Bavaria.

Wagner's past also made him suspect to the conservative Bavarian politicians. Relations between him and Pfistermeister quickly deteriorated. To make matters worse, Ludwig's prime minister between 1864 and 1866, Baron Ludwig von der Pfordten, had served in the Saxon government during the 1849 revolution, an experience that led him to consider Wagner a profoundly evil man. Given Wagner's reputation as a revolutionary, the politicians expected him to have a political agenda, but on this count they had little to fear. While he was never averse to expressing his opinion on any subject, however little he might know about it, Wagner's concept of politics was, as several of his more acerbic opponents observed, purely "operatic," with no understanding of the practical difficulties involved in political administration. In any event, despite his past republican and anarchist associations, Wagner was now a convinced monarchist. He did, of course, have a program. With the full cooperation of Ludwig, he sought to turn Munich into a mecca of Wagnerian art. If any politician offered opposition to this goal, Wagner had no scruples about recommending his dismissal, but he was interested in politics only to the degree that it could support or hinder his art.

The first sign of strain in his relations with the political establishment came in February 1865, when he was refused access to the king, ostensibly over a misunderstanding about payment for a portrait of himself that was a gift to Ludwig. Although the contretemps blew over, the stability of his position was eroded. While political considerations alone were insufficient to arouse public opinion against him, he himself could be trusted to infuriate the Bavarians. The king's generosity allowed him to indulge his craving for luxury to the full, yet Bavaria was not a rich state. For example, the 4,000 gulden that was Wagner's initial allowance was larger than the annual salary paid to the head of a ministerial department after eighteen years of service.[4] This amount was still insufficient to meet his needs and pay off his debts, so, on October 1865, he negotiated a doubling of his allowance and a gift of 40,000 gulden. The treasury forthrightly expressed its distaste for this transaction by paying the money in sacks of coins, which required two cabs to transport from the bank to Wagner's residence. But however extravagant Wagner seemed to the Bavarians, it has been suggested that Ludwig's support of his friend was a pittance by comparison with the extravagant architectual projects of the castles of Linderhof, Neuschwanstein, and Herrenchiemsee, the building of which led to Ludwig's deposition in 1886. Likewise, the total value of money and gifts in kind given to Wagner by Ludwig over the nineteen years of his patronage—562,914 marks—was smaller than the royalty payment of 750,000 marks that Meyerbeer received for one-hundred performances of *Le Prophète* (*The Prophet*) at the Berlin Opera. Nevertheless, Wagner's extravagance, coupled with the arrogance with which he made his demands, lost him much support. Royal favorites have rarely been public idols. In particular, the Bavarians, counter to their image as a sybaritic people, were thrifty and resented the large sums of money being spent on theatre. This factor had led, some years before, to the dismissal of Franz Dingelstedt, the distinguished intendant of the Court Theatre.

Other factors intensified Wagner's unpopularity. Although plans for the music school were slow to materialize and the festival theatre never got beyond the advanced planning stage, Wagner lost no time in importing "foreigners" from other German states to further his plans. This aroused the Bavarian suspicion of outsiders, especially of Protestant Prussians who offended the Catholic sensitivities of Southern Germans. Added to this was sexual scandal. Although the Bülows ostensibly remained man and wife, the liaison between Wagner and Cosima soon became an open secret, and, though Cosima's daughter, Isolde, born on 10 April 1865, had Hans as her nominal father, the actual father was Wagner. Only Ludwig, innocent of any sexual experience at this phase in his life, believed in the purity of the relations between Wagner and the Bülows.

Wagner's downfall was sudden. In mid-November 1865, he spent a week with Ludwig at the alpine castle of Hohenschwangau. On his return to Munich, he ran into a press storm, instigated by hostile politicians. A newspaper article critical of his influence on Ludwig aroused his ire, leading him to publish a furious response. In it, he demanded the dismissal of unnamed but highly placed ministers. The furor caused Ludwig's family and the political establishment to demand Wagner's exile, which Ludwig was reluctantly forced to accept. Early in the morning of 10 December 1865, the composer once again set out on his seemingly aimless wanderings.

In fact, his situation was much better than the one from which Ludwig had saved him. He still received adequate maintenance through the royal stipend. Moreover, Ludwig had assured him of his undying support, which was not an empty promise, and anyway the exile was intended to be for only a few months. Wagner traveled to Lake Geneva, where he took an extended lease on a house, and then moved on to the south of France. Here he received the news of Minna's death in Dresden, an event that moved him, though not sufficiently to persuade him to attend her funeral. In March 1866, he was reunited with Cosima, with whom he traveled through Switzerland after giving up the lease on the Geneva house. Crossing Lake Lucerne, they noticed a large, plain house situated on a promontory, backed by a spectacular view of Mount Pilatus. The secluded house, named Tribschen, seemed an ideal retreat after the stresses of Munich, and Wagner leased it at once. On 15 April, he moved into the house that would be his constant home for the next seven years, where he would complete some of his greatest works and spend some of the happiest and most tranquil days of his life.

His departure from Munich did not mean the end of his relations with Ludwig. For years, the two men engaged in an intense, though irregular, correspondence, notable for the effusiveness with which each expressed his deepest devotion to the other. Although Ludwig entered into homosexual liaisons later in life, it is most unlikely that a similar relationship existed between him and Wagner. Wagner often expressed his aversion to homosexual practices, and florid correspondence such as theirs was more conventional in their own time than in our own. Nevertheless, Ludwig remained deeply dependent on Wagner and, for a time at least, blind to his failings. Soon after Wagner had settled at Tribschen, Ludwig insisted on visiting him to celebrate his birthday, even though a crisis was brewing in Munich over the imminent outbreak of the Austro-Prussian War. Ludwig was coldly received on his return to Munich from Tribschen, and a major newspaper, the *Volksbote*, printed a snidely worded article referring unmistakably to Wagner and Cosima's intimacy. Bülow challenged the editor to a duel, without result, and threatened to resign from the Court Theatre. Since he was Wagner's main connection with the Munich theatre, his departure would be disastrous. Accordingly, Wagner and Cosima insisted that the king write Bülow a letter, actually drafted by Wagner, in which Cosima's name was cleared and also that the king assert his total confidence in the propriety of the Bülow marriage. Ludwig, still believing in Wagner's innocence, did this, and Bülow had the letter published in two of the foremost Bavarian newspapers. Ludwig's credulity about Wagner and Cosima became increasingly strained, until a scandal involving the couple and Malvina Schnorr, who was distraught over her husband's recent death, finally led Ludwig to admit sadly the irregularity of their relationship. While he never lost faith in Wagner the artist, he became acutely aware of the moral fallibility of the man.

The retreat to Tribschen represented only a partial withdrawal by Wagner from his involvement in public affairs and the life of the theatre. Early in 1867, he resumed visits to Munich in connection with further model productions of his work (*Lohengrin* in June and *Tannhäuser* in August 1867) and to protect whatever interests he had in the Court Theatre, which he still saw as the main outlet for his work since the construction of the festival theatre had run into insuperable political obstacles. In fact, these years witnessed a major revival in Wagner's interest in the theatre, preparatory to the founding of the Bayreuth Festival Theatre in the next decade.

Wagner's proximity to the heart of Bavarian political life resulted too in a renewed interest in the function of art in contemporary society, a theme that had been central to his polemical writings of the early 1850s. He undertook a comprehensive treatment of this topic in a series of articles entitled *Deutsche Kunst und deutsche Politik* (*German Art and German Politics*), published between October and December 1867 in the *Süddeutsche Presse*, a journal subsidized by the King and founded specifi-cally for the articulation of Wagnerian views. These articles explored further the dichotomy between France and Germany, a theme that had first emerged in his articles and stories from Paris in the early 1840s and had remained a central concern ever since.

France, Wagner argued, was the preeminent influence upon the political and economic life of modern Europe, which was characterized by its extreme materialism and devotion to making money, no matter what the cost to its integrity and moral well-being. Due to that country's power, French culture enjoyed widespread prestige among foreign rulers, especially German princes. Consequently, French art and fashions had been much imitated, resulting in a modern art that was slick and mechanically effective, but without depth. Although contemporary German culture was still imbued with Frenchness, Wagner considered Germany's mission to be a regeneration of the spirit of Europe through the creation of an art that did not appeal by mere surface attraction and that expressed the aspirations of the Folk. He calls on the German princes, to whom he initially attributed the "Francification" of German culture, to foster the rebirth of Folk culture by founding appropriate institutions—above all, theatres.

Notable in Wagner's renewed polemic was the absence of the model of the Festival of Dionysus, which had been central to his vision of theatre in the early 1850s. Indeed, though he remained aware of theatre as a communal venture, he had now become more concerned about its appeal to the individual. In this, he returned to his earlier definition of German experience as quintessentially an "inward" one and to its art as a phenomenon that had no pragmatic use. To be "German," he claimed, was to do "the thing one does for its own sake and for the joy of doing it" (GSB, XIV, 101). Therefore, by implication, theatre should be devoted less to creating a sense of communal identity within the audience and more toward leading each individual member of that audience to a supreme view of the human condition, free from strictly utilitarian concerns. The revival of the theatre must be the precondition for the revival of the other arts. This would be possible only when theatres were established whose purposes were to transport audiences to a level of consciousness that they could never achieve in life and to create a world in which the highest ideals of the German people might be materialized. This vision was not new, for Wagner cited as his model the Golden Age of German theatre—the age of Lessing, Goethe, and Schiller—before it had been sullied by the triviality of the plays of August von Kotzebue, a highly successful though essentially shallow playwright, whose work enjoyed immense popularity in the first two decades of the nineteenth century. Whereas in that earlier period, theatre had only supported the state, Wagner now conceived of it even more strongly as the central institution that should generate and modify scoiety's consciousness of itself. This did not differ substantially from his vision of theatre that appeared in the theoretical works of his early Zurich days, except for one crucial point. Now he argued that theatre should appeal to each member of the audience not as a public citizen but as a private individual. This redirected appeal carried with it the clear implication that the authority of the artist should ultimately replace that of the state.

Although there was little in this to which Ludwig could object, since he was notably diffident with regard to his own power, Wagner was still able to create turmoil in Munich politics, and the publication of the last two articles of the fifteen in the series was prohibited when he came too close to criticizing the *status quo*. But before writing these articles, he had already completed an infinitely more persuasive deliberation on the function of art within society, his single comic music drama, *Die Meistersinger von Nürnberg* (*The Mastersingers of Nuremberg*). This work, at its first production at the Munich Court Theatre on 21 June 1868, proved, along with *Rienzi*, to be the most popular success of Wagner's career.

Wagner had initially conceived of an opera about the mastersingers back in 1845, when he had been working on *Tannhäuser*. At that time, he had sketched a prose draft of the plot and included a detailed account of it in "A Communication to My Friends." Serious work on it did not start until the winter of 1861–1862, however, when he wrote the poem during a brief stay in Paris. Completion of the score was endlessly delayed, not because inspiration was lacking, but because he rarely found the stability essential for successful composition. Most of act 1 was composed in Biebrich, but it was only completed three-and-a-half years later, soon after his exile from Munich. The bulk of the work was done at Tribschen, act 2 being composed in the summer of 1866 and act 3 over the winter of 1866–1867. The work was finished in its entirety early in March 1867.

The Mastersingers is perhaps the most instantly accessible of Wagner's works. Set in the relatively unproblematic world of late medieval Nuremberg, it is an optimistic piece, with an ending that is close to utopian. Illuminated by a generosity of spirit characteristic of the greatest comic writers, the sheer ingenuity and resourcefulness of the poetry and the bounteous score give the whole work a distinctly Shakespearean quality. The benevolent spirit of *The Mastersingers* is all the more remarkable in that it was written during two notably stressful periods, the first when his career seemed to be in ruins and the second when his dealings with the Munich establishment showed him to be motivated by impulses that were far from either generous or benevolent. No doubt, the constant presence of Cosima had much to do with the uncommonly benign atmosphere of the drama. Nonetheless, while its theme was consistent with much of his thinking about art at that time, its mood was alien to that which characterized his public life. In fact, *The Mastersingers* is a perfect example of how Wagner could use the completeness of his imagination to escape from the hostility of the actual world around him. As he wrote in his diary in 1865:

The world that *I* cannot shape, I must simply forget; it is the only relationship I can have towards it. . . . I must shut myself off from the atmosphere of reality, there is nothing else for it. All else is abuse, destruction—a squandering of my life forces.[5]

Wagner drew on several sources for his material, including the play *Hans Sachs* (1829) by the popular writer and stage director Johann Ludwig Deinhardstein, a light-hearted opera based on the same play (1840) by Albert Lortzing, stories by E.T.A. Hoffmann, and several history books on medieval Germany. Nevertheless, the plot was largely his own invention. A knight, Walther von Stolzing, comes to Nuremberg to join the guild of mastersingers, which is constituted of craftsmen from various trades, all of whom also compose poetry and music according to complex rules. Walther falls in love with Eva, the daughter of Pogner, a wealthy goldsmith and prominent mastersinger, who has determined that his daughter's hand will be bestowed on whichever mastersinger wins a singing competition to be held on Midsummer's Day. Walther tries to join the guild by singing before the assembled mastersingers, but his song, a seemingly formless hymn to nature and love, is rejected by them and especially by the critical town clerk Beckmesser, since it does not seem to obey the rules that the mastersingers insist that all initiates and members must follow in their compositions. Only Hans Sachs, the great cobbler-poet, senses genius in the young man's song. In act 2, which is set in the street outside the houses of Pogner and Sachs, Walther tries to elope with Eva. Their flight is prevented by Sachs and the arrival of Beckmesser, who, eager to win Eva himself, comes to sing a serenade beneath her window. Sachs, who is making shoes, insists on hammering during the serenade, but, after Beckmesser objects, agrees to hammer only when Beckmesser breaks the rules. Sachs finishes his shoes well before Beckmesser finishes his song, and the resulting altercation between the two men ends in a riot in which all the inhabitants of the street turn out to fight. The first scene of the final act is set in Sachs house where Walther has spent the night. Walther tells of a marvelous dream and turns it into a song that fits naturally into the form sanctioned by the mastersingers. While he is dressing for the song contest,

Beckmesser appears and, seeing a copy of the song in Sachs' handwriting, thinks that the poem was written by Sachs. He persuades Sachs to give him a copy so that he can sing it in the contest. Then Eva appears. When Walther returns to the room and catches sight of her, he finishes the song as a declaration of his love for her. The spectacular final scene is the song contest, which takes place after a grand procession of the guilds. Beckmesser performs the song to his own tune, making an appalling travesty of it. Then Walther appears and delivers the final version with such beauty and power that he is spontaneously granted Eva's hand and, after a monologue by Sachs on the sacredness of German art, entry into the guild of the mastersingers.

While Walther and Eva are technically the central characters of the action, they actually figure less prominently than Sachs and Beckmesser, who embody the thematic conflict of the work. Sachs, a poet who respects tradition, values innovation, and sees great art as an expression of the Folk, articulates most clearly Wagner's ideas about the nature and function of art. Walther, unremarkable in himself as a character, is primarily the dramatic embodiment of Sachs' ideas. Beckmesser, based partly on the anti-Wagnerian critic, Eduard Hanslick, is concerned only with rules and restricting the practice of art to a professional elite. The generous spirit of the drama clearly does not extend to him, for he is the absurd pretender to the privileges of the lovers and must be rejected in order for the comic world to be complete. Furthermore, he has no concept of why there are rules in poetry and music, conceiving of them only as means whereby one gains power over others. For Sachs, however, rules have a vital function. As Walther is composing his "Mastersong," Sachs observes that freshness in expressing oneself is easy when one is young, in the springtime of life. The true master can revive the spirit of spring in later, more troubled seasons in life, but only if he has the rules to remind him of his earlier spontaneity. For Sachs, the fullest function of the mastersingers' rules is therefore to guarantee poetry and music as forces that invigorate society and keep its spirit youthful.

It is, of course, the vision of Sachs, not of Beckmesser, that determines the outcome of the action and is embodied in the setting and music. Walther's rhapsodies in act 1 glorify nature as inspiration; in act 2, the magical, midsummer mood is invoked by some of the most ingratiating music Wagner ever wrote. Finally, Walther's prize-song, an evocation of paradise, explicitly associates the creation of poetry with the consummation of love. The action ends with the union of Walther, the new Adam, with his Eve. Through them, art will invigorate and perpetuate the human race.

While *The Mastersingers* dramatized Wagner's current thinking on the social importance of art, it also reflected his nationalism, which had been intensified by his association with Ludwig II, whom he came to see as the prince whose patronage might preserve the art of the German Folk. Nuremberg is a quintessential German town, described by Sachs as a place where tradition is revered and hard work respected; furthermore, its picturesque streets and compact community were a utopia in contrast to the impersonal, corrupting materialism that Wagner never failed to insist was characteristic of the modern world. In 1865, shortly before resuming work on *The Mastersingers*, he had published an essay entitled "Was ist deutsch?" ("What is German?"). Here the term "deutsch" was defined as meaning "what is plain to us, what we rely on, are accustomed to, have inherited from our fathers, what springs from our soil" (*GSB*, XIII, 160). In the mind of Wagner and his audiences, these attributes were perfectly realized in the cozy environment of Nuremberg. Later in the same essay, Wagner gave a more romantic definition of his ideal countryman. "In rugged woods, during the long winter, by the warm hearth-fire of his chamber in a tower that soars high into the air, he tends the memories of his forefathers, shapes the myths of his national gods into inexhaustibly various sagas" (*GSB*, XII, 166–167). These lines unmistakably prefigure Walther's first aria in act 1, "Am stillen Herd" ("By the quiet hearth"), in which he describes the genesis of his artistic inspiration. In the course of the action, Walther, who begins as an untutored nature-poet and the emblem of the inwardness that Wagner considered characteristic of Germans, learns to blend personal expression with the tradition through which the art of the Folk is preserved. Sachs' soliloquy at the end of the drama, in which he calls upon all present to worship German art, turns the story of Walther and Eva into an unmistakable national parable. His closing exhortation, "ehrt Eure deutschen Meister!," has in our own time caused much offense, given the political uses to which *The Mastersingers* was put by the Nazis in the 1930s. But the normal English translation of "honor your German masters!" is inaccurate; a more precise rendering would be "honor your German master craftsmen," which keeps the work within the aesthetic realm where Wagner intended it to remain.

Wagner had not had such a great success since the première of *Rienzi*. This was due in part to the music. In contrast to *Tristan*, *The Mastersingers* is reassuringly diatonic. Furthermore, as befits a drama on the themes of nationality and tradition, he acknowledged the German masters who had come before him. Despite the anachronism, he paid tribute to Bach, whose music can be heard in the chorale that opens the action and in the magnificent rendering of Sachs' poem "Wacht auf" ("Awake!"), sung by the full chorus as he arrives at the song festival. Wagner's contemporaries were perhaps also pleased by his seeming return to a more traditional "numbers" opera. While the music is as continuous as in *The Ring*, solos can be isolated, and there are numerous concerted passages, ranging from duets through to the serene quintet that precedes the final scene. The staggeringly complex ensembles that end acts 1 and 2 demonstrate above all that Wagner himself had learnt the lesson he was teaching through Sachs, showing himself capable of compressing the most diverse and chaotic material within the strict compass of artistic form, and, in the case of act 2, a rigorous fugue. Throughout, he employed the technique of leitmotif as resourcefully as ever, often with brilliantly comic effect.

A further reason for the success of *The Mastersingers* was its familiar theatrical world. The background of the late Middle Ages was loved by audiences bred on grand opera, though, in both music and staging, Wagner represented it with an intimacy and humanity rare in the theatre of his time. In rehearsal, he revealed himself to be a stage director of considerable invention and resource, discovering appropriate gestures for every moment, so that the multitude of incidents comprising the plot were vividly realized and flowed with an ease that none in the audience had previously witnessed. Then too, in contrast with *Tristan*, the entire idiom of *The Mastersingers* fitted rather than strained contemporary stage conventions. As a result, it was soon performed throughout Germany, having been seen by 1870 in Dessau, Karlsruhe, Dresden, Mannheim, Weimar, Vienna, and Berlin (*BaRW*, 182). By contrast, the second production of *Tristan* did not take place until 1876, in Berlin.

On the first night, Wagner took a bow not from the stage, but, by permission of the king, from the royal box. This unprecedented breach of etiquette seemed to herald his return to a position of power and aroused much criticism. In fact, exactly the opposite occurred, for Wagner progressively withdrew from all contact with Munich and its theatre. He did not see Ludwig for another eight years, until the first performance of *The Ring* at Bayreuth. For the next two years, Wagner rarely ventured far beyond Tribschen and its immediate environs. The main reason was that the scandal of his intimacy with Cosima refused to abate, and their need for each other was so acute that they were unable to spend more than a few days apart. Hence, in November 1868, they abandoned the facade of respectability. Cosima came to live permanently with Wagner and insisted on a divorce from Bülow. Her third child by Wagner, Siegfried, was born on 6 June 1869.

Wagner's withdrawal from the theatre was also due to deep differences between him and Ludwig. In the early days of their relationship, Wagner had given Ludwig the legal rights to *The Ring*, which the King now wished to hear. Wagner initially insisted that the tetralogy should first be performed as a whole under festival circumstances. When he heard that the Munich Court Theatre was to undergo substantial renovation, involving the construction of much new machinery, however, he agreed that performances of *The Rhinegold* and *The Valkyrie* could be given there, under the baton of his young disciple, the conductor Hans Richter. As rehearsals for *The Rhinegold* proceeded, however, it was clear that Wagner's control over events in the theatre, which he attempted to exercise from Tribschen, was beginning to slip. Taking advantage of rumors that the technical aspects of the staging were woefully inadequate and might ruin the performance, Wagner insisted that the whole production be stopped until he had personally taken charge. The king became infuriated by the man who constantly flouted his authority, which, despite his diffidence in matters of state, he still prized. Ludwig dismissed Richter, accepted the resignations of those singers who had sided with Wagner, and insisted that the production go ahead with alternative personnel. *The Rhinegold* was eventually performed at the Munich Court Theatre on 22 September 1869, attracting an audience including some of the most prominent musicians of the day, although Wagner himself was not among them. Judging from the reception, the performance was far from the fiasco Wagner had forecast, in spite of realistic scenery was he believed not to be wholly adequate. *The Valkyrie* followed on 26 June 1870, again with an international audience but no Wagner.

In July 1870, Cosima finally obtained a divorce, and she and Wagner were married on 25 August at the Protestant church in Lucerne. Such an event would seem to have guaranteed that the idyllic years spent at Tribschen might continue indefinitely (Illustration 7). But changes in Wagner's plans for *The Ring* were to dictate otherwise. There was now no chance that Munich would be the home for his festival theatre where *The Ring* was to have received its first performance. In March 1870, he and Cosima had read an encyclopedia article on Bayreuth, a small Franconian town in the northern part of Ludwig's territories. The most distinguished building in this town was a beautiful rococo theatre that had been built by the margrave of Bayreuth over a hundred years earlier. This royal city with its splendid theatre, not far from that quintessentially German city of Nuremberg, might be the ideal place to stage the first complete production of *The Ring*.

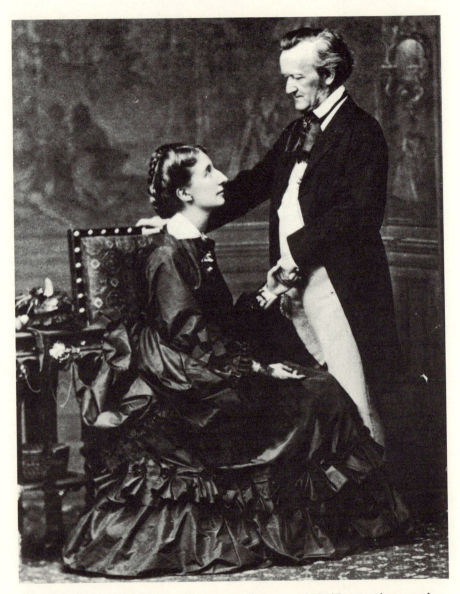

Illustration 7. Richard and Cosima Wagner, Vienna, 1872. (From a photograph by Fritz Luckhardt. Reproduced by permission of the Nationalarchiv der Richard-Wagner-Stiftung/Richard-Wagner-Gedenkstätte, Bayreuth.)

NOTES

1. Richard Wagner, *Selected Letters*, ed. and trans. Stewart Spencer and Barry Millington (London: Dent, 1987), 600.

2. Otto Strabel, ed., *König Ludwig und Richard Wagner Briefwechsel.* 5 vols. (Karlsruhe: Braun, 1936–39), I, 86 (henceforward *LuWB*).

3. Detta Petzet and Michael Petzet, *Die Richard Wagner-Bühne König Ludwigs II* (Munich: Prestel, 1970), 52.

4. Wilfred Blunt, *The Dream King: Ludwig II of Bavaria* (London: Hamish Hamilton, 1970), 29.

5. Richard Wagner. *Das braune Buch: Tagebuchaufzeichnungen 1865–1882*, ed. Joachim Bergfeld (Zürich: Atlantis, 1975), 44.

Chapter 7

The Master of Bayreuth

Wagner's decision to build a theatre specifically for production of *The Ring of the Nibelung* arose from two immediate causes. First, there was no doubt that his credibility with the king had been severely damaged. *The Rhinegold* and *The Valkyrie* had been staged over Wagner's objections, and there were clear signs that the moment the score of *Siegfried* was completed, it would suffer the same fate. If he wished to see the tetralogy performed under conditions he considered ideal, Wagner would need to establish himself on a more independent basis. The second and more positive incentive to build the theatre might have arisen in December 1870, when he read in draft form a small book to be entitled *Die Geburt der Tragödie* (*The Birth of Tragedy*) by the young classical philologist Friedrich Nietzsche.

Although the friendship of Wagner and Nietzsche was to end in hostility, its early years were considered by both men to be among the most fulfilling experiences of their lives. They met in November 1868 during one of Wagner's rare visits to his family in Leipzig. Soon after, Nietzsche was appointed professor of classical philology at Basel University, so he lived within easy reach of Tribschen. From May 1869 up through the departure of the Wagners for Bayreuth in April 1872, he was such a regular visitor that he had his own room at their home. At this stage in their relationship, the two men were entirely at one in their intense idealism and their vision of the capacity of art to save a society corrupted by materialism. "Your life, your writings, and your music," Nietzsche wrote to Wagner soon after their meeting, "are permeated . . . [with] that serious and more spiritual outlook upon life of which we poor Germans have been robbed overnight."[1] Nietzsche, a great stylist, was capable of explaining the historic significance of Wagner's work more eloquently than the composer himself, while his vision of music drama as the salvation of a society crippled by centuries of subservience to the Christian ethos complemented Wagner's view of his own importance.

The Wagners visited Bayreuth in April 1871. At once they determined that the baroque theatre there was inadequate for *The Ring*, but Wagner was so taken by the town, which he pleasurably recalled traveling through in his Magdeburg days, that he decided to make it the site for his festival and his new home. The couple then traveled on to Leipzig and Berlin, where Wagner was inducted into the Royal Academy of Arts and dined with Bismarck, whose political career was reaching its zenith after Prussia's victory in the war with France in 1870. Indeed, the rise of Prussia as the unifying German power contributed to Wagner's choosing to found his festival, since he intended it to exemplify all that was ideal in the German character. His treatment as a celebrity during his visit to northern Germany even encouraged him to think of himself as a national figurehead. Accordingly, in May 1871, he announced that the first Bayreuth Festival, presenting the première of the complete performance of *The Ring*, would take place in the summer of 1873.

The municipality of Bayreuth was highly agreeable to Wagner's plans. The town council voted to give him free land for the building of the theatre; early in 1872, the councilors proved as good as their word when they donated an imposing site on the Bürgerreuth, a hill just fifteen minutes' walk from the center of town. Soon after this, Wagner selected a large plot close to the old royal palace as the site for his new home. Ludwig, despite intensely ambivalent feelings toward the whole project, provided him with funds for building the house, which Wagner named "Wahnfried," a term that translates roughly as "Freedom from Delusion." On 22 April 1872, Wagner left Tribschen for Bayreuth, and Cosima and the children followed a few days later. A saddened Nietzsche helped them through the final days in their much-loved Swiss home. Exactly one month later, on his fifty-ninth birthday, Wagner laid the foundation stone for the new theatre, an occasion later compared by Nietzsche to the unification of Europe and Asia by Alexander.[2]

Unfortunately, the German composer was not as wealthy as the Macedonian king, and funds for the construction of the theatre, estimated at 300,000 thalers, were urgently needed. Again, the town of Bayreuth did not let Wagner down. Friedrich Feustel, a prominent banker, and Theodor Muncker, the mayor, who were both enthusiastic proponents of the Wagnerian cause, formed a management committee to put the operation on a businesslike basis. Their initial idea was to raise money by issuing 1,000 *Patronatscheine*, certificates to be bought by patrons for 300 thalers each, giving them the right to attend the first festival. This scheme was to be administered from Berlin by the Baroness von Schleinitz and Carl Tausig, a gifted young composer. A few months later, Emil Heckel, a music dealer, suggested founding Wagner societies in various German cities so that the less affluent could have a stake in the festival too. But, by the start of 1873, it was clear that neither of these schemes would raise sufficient money. Feustel then suggested that Wagner embark on a series of concerts to raise money, a proposal he greeted with dismay since such tours severely taxed his health, which had never been good. Nevertheless, he went ahead. Eventually, sufficient funds were raised from various sources to allow the external walls of the building to be completed, an occasion marked by a topping-out ceremony early in August 1873, the month that Wagner had initially selected for the first festival. No money was left for stage machinery, scenery, or the decoration of the auditorium.

At this point, Wagner, who had planned to create the whole festival without the help of Ludwig, was forced to appeal once again to his royal patron. His initial plea fell on deaf ears. The king was offended by Wagner's abandonment of Munich as the site for the festival; moreover, his treasury was severely depleted by his own extravagant building projects, the castles of Linderhof and Neuschwanstein. Wagner then appealed to other German rulers. Suggestions even reached the Prussian Kaiser that he might wish to subsidize the first Bayreuth festival as a celebration of the fifth anniversary of Prussia's victory over France. But the Kaiser, like the other German princes, remained indifferent.

It was not until early in 1874 that Ludwig relented and, in a passionate effusion reminiscent of their correspondence in earlier days, stepped in to save the project. "No, no, and no again!" he wrote, "it shall not end this way! Help must be forthcoming! Our plan must not falter. Parcival [Ludwig] knows his mission and will do whatever it lies in his power to do" (*LuWB*, III, 29). In fact, that power was not so great as it had been. The festival management committee was granted 100,000 thalers, but only as a loan, not as a gift. The money was to be paid off by revenue raised from incoming *Patronatscheine* and box-office receipts. Wagner had to continue his concerts to raise more funds, necessitating a grueling tour in the first half of 1875.

Wagner's efforts to establish the Bayreuth Festival were Herculean, sapping his energy to such a degree that his health was permanently impaired and his life probably shortened. Why therefore was he so obsessed to establish the festival and to build, without precedent in modern history, a theatre in the middle of a rural society? The question is worth answering, because the Bayreuth project represents a sustained attempt by Wagner to eradicate those features that made theatre so antipathetic to him. In a broader perspective, the institution of the Bayreuth Festival and the prototype of theatre that it produced have substantially influenced our own understanding of the function of theatre. Moreover, the theatre that Wagner constructed provided a physical prototype that has been utilized by modern theatre architects more frequently than any other model.

The Bayreuth Festival can be regarded as an attempt by Wagner to resolve a longstanding contradiction in his own life. Historically, theatre has been an urban art, because only cities can produce sufficient audiences and funds to support theatres. Wagner hated modern cities and the materialistic civilization they spawned. As we have seen, he considered the theatres for which this society clamored to be capable of providing only trivial entertainment as a diversion from the strains of everyday living. Whether they were commercial or court institutions, theatres had to offer entertainment in such quantity that productions were inevitably routine and lacking in artistic integrity. Furthermore, since audiences took delight in self-display, attention at theatrical events was often focused as much upon people in the auditorium as upon the performers on stage.

Wagner's objections to the theatre of his time were not exclusive to him, and they can still be heard today. His rancor was intensified, however, by a more personal dilemma. As a music dramatist, he could have his work performed only in cooperation with other people and in public, where hundreds, even thousands, of audience members gathered to see it. As we have already seen, he, more intensely than perhaps all other dramatists and composers, was so attached to the works that he created that, from *Rienzi* on, he felt acutely uncomfortable at seeing them represented on stage. He experienced any imperfection, be it an unsympathetic audience or inadequacy in performance or production, as a violation of his very person.

This antipathy to the fundamental conditions of theatre first crystallized in the early days of his exile in Zurich. It informed much of his theoretical writing and disclosed itself specifically in the idea of a festival in his letter to Kietz, where he wrote of a temporary structure of "planks and beams" in a meadow. The theme of a festival theatre continued in his polemical writings and, though details varied from document to document, in essence it remained unchanged. The festival was to be held in a small town far from the corrupting influence of the big city. The theatre was to be no grandiose edifice but a simple structure devoted solely to the effective production and viewing of drama. The utility of its appointments, the lack of decoration, and the possibly temporary nature of its structure were to challenge directly the monumentality that Wagner associated with the urban theatre. Most importantly, all who participated, whether artists or audience, could do so by invitation only. The artists should be in closest sympathy with the composer-dramatist, who would require them to observe the most exact correlation between word, musical tone, mimetic performance, and physical setting, since the seamless harmony of all performative elements was the essential principle of the total work of art. Only under the circumstances of a festival theatre, where artists could be relieved of the stresses of rehearsing and performing a disparate repertoire, could sufficient concentration be found to ensure such correlation down to the minutest detail. As for the audience, it should consist of friends only, for Wagner claimed, not accurately as history would prove, that his dramas achieved clear definition only when witnessed by those who understood him rather than by the mass public, who invariably expected something different. With such controls, Wagner no doubt hoped to lessen the acute pain he felt when he saw his drama inadequately performed before an alien audience and by artists unknown to him. The festival would be an intimate conversation between him and his sympathizers. As he had written to Liszt in 1852,

> As an audience, I can only imagine a collection of friends who have gathered together at some place with the intention of becoming acquainted with my work, preferably in some beautiful wild place, far from the fumes and industrial stench of our urban civilization. (*WLB*, I, 162)

Over twenty years later, his ideas had not changed. With such ambitions, it is not surprising that plans for a festival in Munich failed. In addition to the king's financial difficulties, the urban environment, political intrigue, and public hostility to a festival theatre meant that the city was entirely unsuited to fulfill Wagner's ambitions. In the course of raising money for Bayreuth, he claimed that he had turned down offers that would have assured ample funding if he had only agreed to build in Berlin or Vienna, but the rural fastness of Bayreuth was fundamental to his whole idea of a festival.

While there were strong personal motives for building the Bayreuth theatre, Wagner and his associates also conceived of the festival as a powerful counterforce to the most destructive qualities of modern society. Nietzsche was an especially eloquent advocate of this function. Although, by 1874, cracks were beginning to appear in the friendship that would eventually lead to Nietzsche's disavowal of all that Wagner stood for, the relationship was cordial until 1876. Only a few weeks before the festival opened in August 1876, Nietzsche published, as the last of his *Unzeitgemässe Betrachtungen* (*Untimely Meditations*), an essay entitled "Richard Wagner in Bayreuth," which remains the most articulate justification of the festival. Although there is evidence that Wagner did not share Nietzsche's views, his initial reading elicited the response, "Friend! Your book is tremendous!—Where did you learn so much about me?" (*NWC*, 267).

Nietzsche represented Wagner as profoundly disaffected by contemporary society, where money was the god of the age, vulgarity reigned, and art was either a luxury for the wealthy or, when purveyed to the masses, a means of making the worker "serviceable, base, and less natural." Theatre, the most social of art forms, was especially debased. It was characterized, Nietzsche argued, by

> strangely clouded judgment, ill-dissembled thirst for amusement, for distraction at any cost, scholarly considerations, pomposity and affectation on the part of performers, brutal greed for money on that of the proprietors, vacuity and thoughtlessness on that of a society which thinks of the people only insofar as [they are] employable or dangerous to it and attends concerts and the theatre without any notion of possessing a duty towards them. (*NUM*, 210)

In contrast, Wagner, the "dithyrambic dramatist," would offer the German nation an art that would restore an authentic language capable of shattering the tyrannical clichés of the time, would reawaken people's awareness of their primordial nature, would rekindle a sense of the tragic, and would arouse a hunger for art as the essential expression of their common need as a Folk. "Bayreuth," Nietzsche announced, "signifies the morning consecration on the day of battle." In fact, Wagner was less interested than he had been in the revolutionary purport of his work; temporarily at least, he was more in accord with the prevailing norms of society than Nietzsche was prepared to recognize. Nevertheless, the essay captures well the most extreme ambitions of Wagner's growing body of followers.

Central to the Bayreuth Festival was the new theatre, which would be perfect for the performance of *The Ring* and neutralize the negative aspects of theatregoing against which Wagner had inveighed. Detailed plans for a festival theatre in Munich had been drawn up and a model had been constructed by Semper, but due to the demise of that project, the architect and composer were no longer on speaking terms. Wagner extracted from these plans whatever he claimed was based on his own ideas; then, in cooperation first with the Berlin architect Wilhelm Neumann and later with the Leipzig architect Otto Brückwald and the theatre technologist Carl Brandt, he designed a strikingly efficient theatre. In contemporary prints, the starkness of the fly-tower, the barnlike structure of the whole, and the isolated setting are reminiscent of the early Elizabethan theatre (Illustration 8). Nothing could have been further from the classical monumentality of the German court theatres. The playhouse was true to the simple German virtues as Wagner hads always conceived them.

The interior was simple too but more care was devoted to it, for here the crucial performance would occur. Wagner sustained his interest in the technical aspects of theatre during the period of planning the festival through a series of essays on performance, the most notable of which, "Über Schauspieler und Sänger" ("On Actors and Singers"), was published soon after the laying of the foundation stone. This polemical survey of German acting was based on the assumption that the illusion created by performance must be so complete that the audience could lose itself within it. "Strictly speaking, art ceases to be art when it strikes our reflecting consciousness as *art*" (*GSB*, XII, 315–316). For Wagner, the ideal performer was the romantic actor Ludwig Devrient, who, in roles such as King Lear, could so transport the audience that, after the performance, the members needed several hours to return to normal consciousness. Most German actors, Wagner claimed, were incapable of exercising such an influence, mainly because they imitated the French, once again put up as a yardstick for all that was inauthentic in modern culture. On stage, the French consciously played roles; each appearance was a strategy, a playing with the audience. German actors copied this but did so against both the spirit of the plays in which they acted and the taste of German audiences who, Wagner asserted, wanted greater honesty. They wanted actors to forget they were actors, to transform themselves into the roles that they assumed. Since this was not happening, German acting was a confused compromise of actors representing roles in an irrelevant fashion, amid conventions that meant nothing to the audience. Wagner wished to create a theatre, spoken and musical, in which this compromise was avoided, a theatre true to the German desire for warm communication, a theatre that was in effect, de-theatricalized.

Essential to this concept of theatre was an auditorium in which the audience's attention would be focused exclusively on the stage and not partially on itself, which is what occurred in the Italian opera house. There the vertical tiers of boxes, arranged in horseshoe style, provided an

Illustration 8. Bayreuth Festival Theatre, exterior, 1873. (From a painting by Louis Sauter. Reproduced by permission of the Nationalarchiv der Richard-Wagner-Stiftung/Richard-Wagner-Gedenkstätte, Bayreuth.)

architectural paradigm almost universally adopted in nineteenth-century Europe. One exception was the theatre in Riga where Wagner had conducted as a young man. In it, the auditorium was raked in a steep amphitheatre and the orchestra pit was considerably lower than in most opera houses. As a result, the illusion shed from the stage was intensified. With the Riga opera house and classical models of theatrical auditoria in mind, Wagner and his colleagues designed an unusual theatrical space (Illustration 9). The orchestra pit was sunk beneath the stage, so that the immense sounds produced by so many instruments were modified, allowing the singers to be heard above them. Also, the small space between the hood that hid the orchestra from the spectators' view and the front of the stage brought the action closer to the audience than in the average opera house, a closeness made even more effective by the absence of light from the music stands. The auditorium was raked and shaped as a wedge rather than constructed in the semicircular or horseshoe style of the usual opera house. This provided unimpeded sightlines from all places in the house, while the arrangement of the seats in unbroken rows did not segregate classes as the Italian opera house did. The only evidence of privilege took the form of the boxes at the back of the house, occupied by royal visitors, other dignitaries, and the Wagner family. But the crowning achievement of the auditorium was the composition of the sidewalls. As Wagner explained, this new auditorium changed the spectator's relation to the scenic picture: "As soon as he has taken his seat, he actually finds himself in a 'theatron,' which is a room intended for nothing else than for looking, in fact for looking at the place dictated by his seat" (*GSB*, XII, 291). The walls of the theatron could not be lined with boxes, since these would distract the attention of the audience in the main body of the house. Still, unadorned walls in place of boxes would be aesthetically unpleasing and therefore equally disturbing. Wagner and his collaborators eventually solved the problem by repeating along the sidewalls of the auditorium the double proscenium that already framed the stage and the opening to the orchestra pit.

> So that the narrowing auditorium accorded completely with the perspective view of the stage, we repeated the principle of the stage throughout the entire auditorium, adding proscenium to proscenium until it reached its culmination in the crowning gallery and thereby included the audience, in whatever seat they were sitting, in the perspective of proscenia. To do this, proscenia were built at each exit, laid out as a widening order of columns at the end of the rows of seats. (*GSB*, XII, 293)

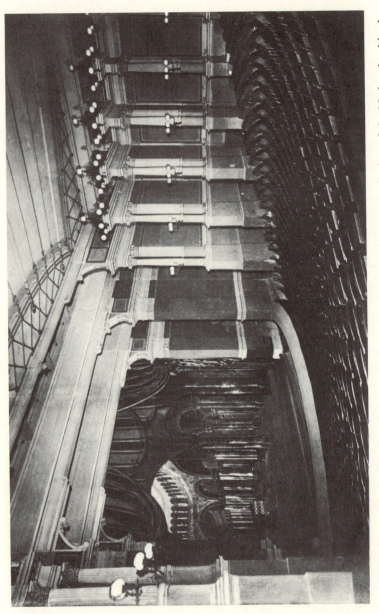

Illustration 9. Bayreuth Festival Theatre, interior, 1882. (Reproduced by permission of the Nationalarchiv der Richard-Wagner-Stiftung/Richard-Wagner-Gedenkstätte, Bayreuth.)

What Wagner had achieved was a neutralization of the power of the audience. By unifying the focus on the stage, the performance, not its own presence in the theatre, became the audience's sole concern. The narrowing of the proscenia toward the stage amplified its sense of being physically bound to the production. In such a configuration, the distance between performance and spectator, which had caused Wagner such anguish earlier in his career, was minimized, and the illusion shed from the stage was complete.

Of course, the most important prerequisite for a successful festival was the completion of *The Ring* itself. With the exception of some orchestration on *Siegfried* in 1864–1865, Wagner had not touched the score since laying down his pen in 1857. He started work on *Siegfried* again in March 1869, before he had any notion of moving to Bayreuth. Although he completed the score of act 3 in Augsut 1869, he delayed putting the finishing touches to it until February 1871, so that he would not have to hand it over to the king, as legally he was obligated to do. By this time, he was well embarked on *Twilight of the Gods*, which he had started in October 1869. Composition continued during the move to Bayreuth and the early years of raising funds for the theatre. This music drama was not completed until 21 November 1874, more than a year after the date originally set for the first festival.

It is remarkable how easily Wagner seems to have picked up the threads of a work that he had abandoned twelve years earlier. No doubt it was never far from his mind, for he had always intended to complete it. Nevertheless, the continuity of act 3 of *Siegfried* with the earlier writing is striking, a testimony to the graphic leitmotifs from which the score had been created. But while the leitmotifs are consistent, much of the music has a different quality. The orchestral writing is more densely textured, the dramatic momentum more urgent, and, while the "unending melody" of the earlier *Ring* is still the prevailing idiom, sections are more formal in structure, reminiscent of the medium of grand opera from which Wagner had initially intended to escape.

Act 3 of *Siegfried* dramatizes Siegfried's ascent of the mountain to claim the sleeping Brünnhilde who is ringed by fire. In order to do this, he must defeat Wotan in the guise of the Wanderer, and this time, the sword, wielded by Siegfried, breaks the god's spear, a moment symbolic of the rise of heroic man, potentially independent of the gods. The love duet that ensues after Siegfried awakens Brünnhilde is the most utopian passage in the cycle, for briefly the love of man and woman seems to have the potential to change the world. Wagner returned to his work at precisely the point in the story where the optimistic philosophy that had first impelled him toward the subject is most completely realized. Siegfried and Brünnhilde, singing together as no two major characters have done so far, reach a rapturous climax just as reminiscent of the great set pieces of romantic grand opera as of the earlier *Ring*. This does not indicate a regression from the theories of the 1850s but demonstrates that Wagner had developed a more versatile technique and a more catholic view as to how dramatic effect could be created through music.

In contrast to *Siegfried, Twilight of the Gods* is grim. The most powerful drama in the cycle, it comes closest in theme, form, and atmosphere to ancient Greek tragedy. As composition progressed, Wagner became increasingly confident that a performance of the cycle would be possible, and, as if in recognition of this, made this last work vividly the most theatrical work of *The Ring*, with dramatic contrasts, passionate confrontations, and plentiful opportunities for picturesque stage settings. Wagner, who had started *The Ring* as a denial of theatre, ended it in acceptance: "It begins in flight from the theatre and ends in a return to it" (*BeRW*, 450). In a curiously inverse manner, the origin of the drama underlines this, for while *Twilight of the Gods* was the last drama to be composed, its poem was the first to be written, under the title *Siegfried's Death*. Hence, it displays theatrical qualities characteristic of the *Lohengrin* period. The action is precisely constructed. At the start, exposition is provided by the three Norns, who recall the past and foretell the cataclysm to come, giving everything that follows clarity and direction. After Siegfried leaves Brünnhilde to become embroiled in the politics of the Gibichung tribe, the epic material is tightly plotted. Wagner had no compunction about using tricks familiar from the popular drama of the time. Siegfried, for example, is drugged by a love potion and adopts a disguise to drag Brünnhilde from the mountain to marry Gunther. His death is the result of a network of misunderstandings that would not be out of place in the most skillfully plotted well-made play.

Although some characters have divine or supernatural origins and powers, *Twilight of the Gods* is the most human drama of the cycle. The gods themselves are absent. When they are mentioned, it is as beings who no longer have a determining influence on events but are worshipped as figures or even figments of the past. Act 2 begins with the Nibelung dwarf Alberich urging his son Hagen, the baleful power behind the Gibichung throne, to destroy all happiness. This scene and the grim wedding festivities that follow are set among altars dedicated to Wotan, Fricka, and Donner. Worship of these gods is now sensed as regressive, a manifestation of the superstitious beliefs of a society ruled by those who crave wealth and political power. The drama resolves itself into a conflict between these regressive forces and the individual who acts with freedom of will. The tragedy resides in the inability of such freedom to survive. While Siegfried is prominent in the action, being the first to fall victim to the ruthless machinations of Hagen, he is no longer pivotal. Instead, like the Gibichung princelings, Gunther and Gutrune, he is a helpless pawn of Hagen, a victim of forces that he cannot understand. His heroism, so effective in a natural environment, is defenseless when faced with the deceptive appearances of human affairs. The dramatic conflict is actually sustained throughout by Hagen and Brünnhilde. Hagen, though not one of Wagner's most complex creations, is among the most impressive. A totally malevolent figure, he is a monster of repression, bound to others solely by his hatred of them. All the same, Wagner makes him oddly attractive, if not wholly sympathetic. The scene with his father Alberich strikes us as a descent into the deepest recesses of the mind, a primordial stratum that is disturbingly familiar. In contrast, Brünnhilde emerges as the tragic hero of the drama. She moves through painful suffering, brought on by Siegfried's betrayal, toward an anagnorisis of classical proportions as she achieves an understanding of the entire history that has led to the final cataclysm. Her act of self-immolation on Siegfried's funeral pyre represents the supreme act of self-sacrifice. While not as positive a gesture as the union of the lovers that ends *Siegfried*, the altruism generated by her love (which Wagner considered vital for the salvation of the world) and the freedom with which she sacrifices herself, make her death more affirmative than the comparatively will-less sacrifices of some of Wagner's earlier heroines. Its glory is reflected in the great final leitmotif of love and rebirth that sounds over the heads of the stunned crowds who have survived the destruction of three generations of human and superhuman history.

The immensity of the theme is complemented by an immensity of resources, especially in the orchestra. *Twilight of the Gods* exemplifies the popular image of Wagnerian music drama, with heavy orchestration in which brass instruments are especially prominent and a decibel level that intensifies to almost intolerable proportions. The orchestra does not provide as precise a realization or commentary on the drama as it does earlier in *The Ring*. It has been estimated that while there are 405 independent occurrences of leitmotifs in *The Valkyrie*, in *Twilight of the Gods*, which is about 50 minutes longer, there are 1,005 (*RWSA*, 105). Consequently, the audience has no chance to recognize, let alone absorb and understand, each leitmotif. So, while he maintained the leitmotivic method, Wagner depended more on the symphonic nature of the orchestra. Early on, dramatic conflict is apparent in the contrast between passages of exuberant joy and somber heaviness, which transforms into barbaric violence as the action progresses. Notable are extended orchestral interludes, such as "Siegfried's Journey to the Rhine," in which crucial transitions in the events and mood of the action are realized, or "Siegfried's Funeral March," an overwhelmingly gloomy meditation on the passing of heroes. Equally striking is Wagner's seeming return to the grand concerted ensemble, characteristic of his pre-*Ring* operas and *The Mastersingers*. Hagen's summoning of the vassals and their welcome of Brünnhilde, the only choral passages in the cycle, disconcertingly blend warlike ritual and raucous humor, while the trio of revenge sung by Brünnhilde, Gunther, and Hagen at the end of act 2 provides as formal ending to the act as the very different duet that completes *Siegfried*. Finally, Brünnhilde's immolation, with its mighty orchestral conclusion, surpasses in spirit the grandest of grand operas. The formality of the music is essential to the appeal of the drama. In contrast to the free-flowing music of the earlier works, this display of form has an archaic quality that stands effectively for the forces of the past that entrap Brünnhilde and Siegfried, but from which Brünnhilde eventually frees herself. In *Twilight of the Gods*, Wagner provided, in the words of Nietzsche, "the supreme model for all art in the grand manner" (*NUM*, 205).

A work of such length and scope as *The Ring*, which makes tremendous demands on singers' vocal power, requires a cast of exceptional artists, so, late in 1872, Wagner and Cosima undertook a tour of German opera houses to discover outstanding singers whom they might invite to perform at Bayreuth. The tour was a depressing experience, turning up only one singer for a minor role and exposing the Wagners to a series of productions they found inept; only Gluck's *Orpheus and Eurydice* at Dessau came fully up to their exacting standards. Nevertheless, by dint of hard work, by exercising his considerable powers of persuasion, and by capitalizing upon his international fame, Wagner managed over the next three years to assemble a cast that included some of the best singers in Germany. Among these were Albert Niemann, the recalcitrant Paris Tannhäuser, for Siegmund, Franz Betz, a Berlin baritone, for Wotan, and the Viennese soprano Amalia Materna for Brünnhilde. Several roles were difficult to cast, above all Siegfried, which was eventually sung by the unknown tenor, Georg Unger.

Because Wagner intended the Bayreuth production of *The Ring* to serve as a model for subsequent productions elsewhere, every detail had to be carefully prepared. Sets were designed by Josef Hoffmann, a Viennese landscape painter who was not a regular set designer, constructed by the workshop of the Brückner brothers in Coburg, and installed by Carl

Brandt, who invented elaborate machines for spectacular effects. A year before the festival, which was eventually set for August 1876, the artists, who were paid only their expenses, gathered for the summer to be personally coached by Wagner in separate rehearsals for singers, orchestra, and technicians.

Final rehearsals began early in June 1876. These provided the most extended opportunity that Wagner had ever had to realize on stage the ideals of the total work of art. The historic nature of these rehearsals was recognized by associates of Wagner, who recorded in detail his instructions to the singers in terms of musical interpretation and stage performance. From all accounts, throughout his life, Wagner was extraordinarily skilled as an actor and reader. Now he had the opportunity to demonstrate that he was a resourceful director too, whose vitality filled his actors with a corresponding energy. His fertile imagination allowed him to improvise several alternative stage situations, the most suitable of which he then chose. Above all, he was concerned that the singers bear themselves on stage as naturally as possible. Heinrich Porges recorded that Wagner discouraged a "coldly objective, elegant, formal" demeanor and insisted that none of the singers indulge in "false pathos or mannerism."[3] In trying to create "a faithful, deeply felt *representation of life* as we experience it" (*PWRR*, 26), he did not demand crass naturalism. Rather, in the classical tradition of German acting, stemming from Lessing's aesthetics of acting as expounded in the *Hamburg Dramaturgy* (1768), he coaxed his actors into maintaining a balance between restraint and passion, urging them to abandon the conventional gestures of operatic acting. They were also forbidden to look out into the audience, with one exception. At the end of *Siegfried*, the lovers were to behave not as if they were communicating with each other, but as if "they are addressing the whole world" (*PWRR*, 114), a striking breach in style that would underline the utopian quality of the duet. Wagner's eminence at Bayreuth meant that his authority as stage director superseded that of Hans Richter, the conductor, and he used it to stipulate that staging considerations should take precedence over purely musical ones. The orchestra should never overcome the singers—a constant danger, especially in *Twilight of the Gods*—but should support them, "as the sea does a boat, rocking but never upsetting or swamping" (*PWRR*, 13). The rhythm, Wagner insisted, should always be modified by the need to create dramatic effect.

Three performances of the complete *Ring*-cycle were given in the Bayreuth theatre in August 1876 (Illustration 10). By now, Wagner was the most famous German of his day, even more widely known than Bismarck, according to some writers. While this celebrity had not enabled

Illustration 10. The first night of *The Rhinegold*, Bayreuth, August 1876. (After a sketch by L. Bechstein. Reproduced by permission of the Nationalarchiv der Richard-Wagner-Stiftung/Richard-Wagner-Gedenkstätte, Bayreuth.)

him to raise ample funds for the festival, it attracted a considerable public who flocked to the small town. But this was not the audience he had initially envisaged. Financial realities meant that he could not make free seats available to whoever wished to attend, as he had originally hoped, so his audience was far from being composed of sympathetic friends or representatives of the mythic Folk for whom he had considered himself to be writing. High prices at the box office precluded all but the wealthy audiences who patronized the court theatres. Thus, his audience was drawn from the classes prospering from the economic expansion that accompanied the unification of Germany under Bismarck—ironically, those very classes that embodied the values explicitly condemned in *The Ring*. Though some noted musicians and artists attended, several did not, a fact seized upon by the press, which, as with most of Wagner's undertakings, had been unceasingly hostile toward the whole festival. Meanwhile, Bayreuth became a tourist trap, touting Richard Wagner souvenirs in a mode that anticipated the commerce of modern times. Although the town could provide most of its visitors with beds, meals were in chronically short supply, a subject that became a more frequent topic of conversation than *The Ring* itself.

A complete performance of *The Ring* had always been the goal of Ludwig's patronage of Wagner. Although he remained cool about Wagner's defection to Bayreuth, the king could not deny himself the pleasure of seeing the work he had done so much to foster. By now, Ludwig was shy to the point of morbidity and unwilling to attend a performance in the presence of the public or royal guests, so he would only attend the general (or final dress) rehearsal in a totally empty theatre. Furthermore, he ordered the train that carried him to Bayreuth to stop in a forest before the station, where he was met by a carriage and transported incognito to one of the Bayreuth palaces where he spent the night conferring with Wagner. On 6 August, he attended the general rehearsal of *The Rhinegold* and then asked that the theatre be filled for the remaining dramas for acoustical reasons. He was overwhelmed by the work. "Happy century!" he wrote to Wagner on his return from Bayreuth, "that saw such a spirit arise in its midst! How coming generations will envy all those whose incomparable good fortune it was to be your contemporaries" (*LuWB*, III, 83). He even returned for the third cycle and ordered a fourth to be given in September, although that proved impossible as by that time all artistic personnel had left. In contrast with Ludwig's secretiveness, the German Kaiser, accompanied by a retinue of petty royalty, bestowed his presence on the first cycle, entering Bayreuth in a royal parade in which Wagner was prominently featured.

The critical reception of *The Ring* was mixed. The more judicious reviewers admitted to being puzzled by the unusual idiom and the lack of several of the most familiar features of grand opera. Some admitted to being confused by the number and density of the leitmotifs, which did not allow them to follow the action as easily as they could in *Tannhäuser* or *Lohengrin*, still Wagner's most popular works. Several found the four evenings overlong, since, with the exception of *The Rhinegold*, each performance lasted a good six hours each. There were likewise mixed reports on the staging. Despite Brandt's ingenious machines and the immense investment in lighting equipment—there were 3,246 gas lights on stage, so that a gas plant had to be built especially for the theatre (*PRWB*, 236)—not all effects worked well. The first cycle was marred by innumerable faults, but the second was, by general consensus, executed with greater efficiency. The auditorium was completely darkened, one of the first times that this had occurred in the European theatre, so the impact of the effects and the lights was heightened. Some critics felt that a total illusion had been successfully created, and others did not. Among the most novel of the stage effects was the use of swimming machines for the Rhine Daughters and of projections in the scene beneath the Rhine; the use of colored steam to hide the scenic transformations also aroused much comment. Several of the effects were, however, half-hearted. It was, for example, impossible to surround Brünnhilde entirely with magic fire, and the dragon specially constructed for Bayreuth by a London firm, was dreadful, especially because part of his neck never arrived, having been sent to Beirut in Lebanon! Claims were made that such things were done better in Paris and London. Indeed, the incomplete execution created an aura of shabby theatricality, which was precisely what these model productions were supposed to have avoided.

As far as production and design were concerned, the first Bayreuth Festival was far from exceptional in its time, which accounts for much of the disappointment in the critical reaction. As a composer of music for the stage, as the initiator of a modern festival theatre, and as a participant in the design and construction of the physical theatre to house it, Wagner's contribution to theatrical history was nothing short of revolutionary. While he was resourceful, imaginative, and precise as a stage director, however, he made no contribution that changed audiences' understanding of the theatre or made them see differently, in the way that his music made them hear differently. Visually, he was unable to go beyond the stylistic modes of his time (Illustration 11), and these modes had already been fully explored in the contemporary German

Illustration 11. The awakening of Brünnhilde, act 3 of *Siegfried*. (Set design by Josef Hoffmann, Bayreuth, 1876. Reproduced by permission of the Nationalarchiv der Richard-Wagner-Stiftung/Richard-Wagner-Gedenkstätte, Bayreuth.)

theatre. Production standards as a whole had improved in the thirty years since his first operas had been produced, due in part to the work of régisseurs that was regarded as exemplary to the German theatre. Laube, Wagner's youthful associate, had developed standards of ensemble acting to an unprecedentedly high level during his tenure as intendant of the Vienna Burgtheater in the 1850s and 1860s. Soon after he resigned from that post in 1867, it was taken over by Dingelstedt, who had previously been intendant of the Munich Court Theatre and the Weimar Court Theatre, where he had made his name with opulent productions of opera, including *Tannhäuser* in Munich, classic German drama, and Shakespeare. Dingelstedt was celebrated for spectacular productions in which romantic scenery and the fluid staging of crowd scenes were attractively combined. Indeed, as a stage director, Dingelstedt more completely and successfully achieved the seamless, total work of art than Wagner did. The preeminent director in the German theatre of the 1870s was, however, the Duke of Saxe-Meiningen, whose famous company specialized in producing German and European classics in settings and costumes that were claimed to be historically accurate. From 1874 on, when the Meininger first appeared in Berlin with its noted production of *Julius Caesar*, its work became the epitome for ensemble performance because the massive crowd scenes and complex spectacle it created on stage was done with attention being paid to the tiniest detail.

While Wagner's production of *The Ring* clearly appealed to the historicist tastes of audiences who required realistic spectacle and the minute reconstruction of historical periods, the sheer length of the cycle, the diversity of its scenes, and the technical challenge of some of the more specialized effects meant that sufficient attention could not be paid to every detail of stage representation and the complementarity of music, word, and gesture. Consequently, much of the production appeared somewhat inadequate, perhaps even passé, for audiences who had seen performances in a similar style in larger cities. Ironically, despite the formidable technical virtuosity of the festival theatre, Wagner was caught in the same dilemma in which, twenty-five years before, he claimed the Zurich theatre had been trapped. Namely, he was imitating the work of nationally celebrated theatres without the resources finally to pull it off to everybody's satisfaction.

Nevertheless, despite the shortcomings of the *Ring* production, even Wagner's enemies finally had to admit that the phenomenon of the Bayreuth Festival was, as the creation of a single man, an achievement unequaled in modern history.

NOTES

1. *Nietzsche-Wagner Correspondence*, ed. Elizabeth Foerster-Nietzsche, trans. Caroline V. Kerr (New York: Liveright, 1921), 12 (henceforward *NWC*).

2. Friedrich Nietzsche, *Untimely Meditations*, trans. R. J. Hollingdale (Cambridge: Cambridge University Press, 1983), 199 (henceforward *NUM*).

3. Heinrich Porges, *Wagner Rehearsing the Ring: An Eye-Witness Account of the Stage Rehearsals of the First Bayreuth Festival*, trans. Robert L. Jacobs (Cambridge: Cambridge University Press, 1983), 3–4 (henceforward *PWRR*).

Chapter 8

The Dying Magus

Two weeks after the close of the festival, when the Wagners left Bayreuth for a holiday in Italy, there was every indication that they intended to hold a second festival in 1877. This would give Wagner an opportunity to correct the faults that had marred the initial *Ring* performances. While they were in Italy, however, Feustel sent news that the deficit was much larger than anyone had anticipated, almost 150,000 marks. Still on holiday, Wagner suggested schemes by which the money could be recouped, whether by a renewed appeal to the patrons or a plan whereby Prussia or Bavaria might take over the festival and run it as a national theatre. But none of these succeeded, for the commercial and political worlds proved to be indifferent to the fate of Wagner's enterprise. Soon after returning to Bayreuth in December 1876, he accepted that the 1877 festival would not take place. In actual fact, the theatre did not reopen until 1882.

Wagner, never one to admit defeat, continued to work to save the festival. Encouraged by reports from a London music agency that he might make a fortune giving concerts in the newly constructed Albert Hall, he traveled in May 1877 to the British capital with an entourage of Bayreuth artists, intending to give twenty concerts to capacity houses of 10,000 each. Unfortunately, only six concerts could be arranged, and, while they attracted large audiences, the revenue they generated was minimal and did nothing to pay off the Bayreuth deficit. While the Wagners' visit to London was a financial fiasco, it was an artistic and social success. The concerts were received with enthusiasm and gave the British an extended introduction to Wagner's music, which prepared for the flood of his music dramas onto the London stage in the early 1880s. Cosima, who spoke excellent English, struck up an intimate acquaintance with George Eliot (Mary Ann Evans) and George Henry Lewes and became friendly with the painter Edward Burne-Jones. In addition, Queen Victoria, while she did not attend the concerts, granted Wagner an audience at Windsor Castle.

Back in Bayreuth, a meeting of twenty Wagner Societies was held in September. Here the composer announced plans to found a school in Bayreuth designed to train performers in his works and "to enable them to perform intelligently and correctly similar works of a genuinely German style" (GSB, II, 331). Future festivals, which would arise from the work of this school, would include performances of all his work from The Flying Dutchman on. Since no progress was made toward paying off the debt, however, plans for the school were soon abandoned. In fact, Germany continued to be so indifferent to the festival that more than once Wagner seriously considered emigrating to the United States. In the end, he was once again saved for Europe by Ludwig. Legally, all his works could be performed in the Munich Court Theatre without payment of royalties, but, because that theatre was profiting handsomely from this arrangement, the king, acting on a suggestion from Cosima, decided that it would be only fair that 10 percent of the box-office receipts from all Wagner performances should go toward paying off first the deficit and then the advance of 1874. This agreement, signed on 31 March 1878, also granted Wagner the right to use the personnel of the Munich Court Theatre for the production of Parsifal, then planned for Bayreuth in the summer of 1880. In return, Munich would have unrestricted rights to perform that music drama.

While the festival was thus saved, Wagner's confidence in it was shaken. No doubt this was due in part to the defection of Nietzsche from the ranks of his supporters. As early as 1874, there were signs in Nietzsche's private notes that his faith in Wagner was wavering. He suspected Wagner's motives and the quality of his work, writing that he "endeavors to tyrannize by the aid of the theatre-going masses," while his work seemed to be crudely populist.

Wagner brings together all possible effective elements at a time when popular taste is dulled and demands extremely crass and vigorous methods. Everything is employed—the magnificent, the intoxicating, the bewildering, the grandiose, the frightful, the clamorous, the ecstatic, the neurotic. Prodigious dimensions, prodigious resources. (NWC, 202)

Even in his major tribute, "Richard Wagner in Bayreuth," Nietzsche threw doubts on the integrity of Wagner's mission, which he found to be the expression "of his obscure personal will, which longed insatiably for *power and fame*" (*NUM*, 227). Added to this, Nietzsche was alienated by the commercialism associated with the festival and the gross materialism of the audiences, who were far from the select band of ardent idealists envisioned at the laying of the foundation stone in 1872. Moreover, while ill health had forced Nietzsche to spend most of the festival away from Bayreuth, the rehearsals and performances that he actually saw did not provide the transcendent experience he had anticipated. In essence, his increasingly hostile critique of Wagner discloses how far the composer had moved from being the castigator of a materialistic society to becoming a representative of it. No doubt Nietzsche was partially averse to his former idol's passion for luxurious living, but Wagner's desire to dominate and the distinct cult of personality associated with the Bayreuth Festival were uncomfortably characteristic of the oppressive social milieu of Bismarckian Germany. While the indifference of that society to his endeavors ultimately guaranteed Wagner's status as an outsider, he did not shrink from exploiting whatever privileges it might accord him.

Wagner and Nietzsche met for the last time in Sorrento in November 1876. Wagner did not seem to be aware of differences between them, but Nietzsche was deeply offended by Wagner's plans for *Parsifal*, which he read as selling out to the slavish beliefs of Christianity. Further relations between the two were not helped by Wagner's tactless suggestion to Nietzsche's doctor that the young philosopher's health problems were caused by excessive masturbation; the split was widened by the publication early in 1878 of *Menschliches, Allzumenschliches (Human, All Too Human)*. Wagner, sensing hostility, did not read the book. Had he done so, he might have understood that the division between them was caused not only by the natural growth to independence of Nietzsche's powerful intellect but also by the very nature of that intellect, which was inimical to Wagner's conception of the function of art in modern society. Though Wagner was never mentioned by name, he was undoubtedly the artist that Nietzsche had in mind throughout the polemic. Nietzsche doubted the value of any art, which he came to consider to be merely play with attractive surfaces that encouraged unclear thinking and undermined "intellectual probity." Art, he insisted, necessarily looks to the past for appeal; the artist is thus retarded, "halted at games that pertain to youth and childhood." Nietzsche assaulted both the cult of genius, enshrined in the Bayreuth project, and the power of artists, "by virtue of which they render men will-less and sweep them away into the delusion that the leaders they are following are supra-natural."[1]

Nietzsche's full hostility was expressed only after Wagner's death. Few themes were as important to him as the composer's work and influence. Later attacks, especially those in *Der Fall Wagner* (*The Case of Wagner*) and *Nietzsche contra Wagner* (both 1888), were based on the assumption that Wagner was a decadent artist nurturing the anxieties of a sick age. Nietzsche also idealized lightness and expressed a belief in the supernal nature of humanity that he ultimately considered necessary qualities to make art an acceptable undertaking. He suspected theatre as inherently corrupt, catering to the vanity of artists, and involving the manipulation of audiences. In essence, Nietzsche's developing Apollonian vision could not comprehend the Dionysian function of Wagnerian theatre that he himself had historically defined in his youthful *Birth of Tragedy*. No doubt, Nietzsche's attachment to the vision of this early book made him experience the loss of Wagner's friendship as the loss of youth. He always recalled those days in Tribschen as the happiest of his life, "those days of mutual confidence, of cheerfulness, of sublime flashes—the *deep* moments" (*NWC*, ix).

Not only did financial problems and Nietzsche's apostasy dent Wagner's confidence in Bayreuth, but the very need for the festival was also brought into question as *The Ring* was soon taken up by other theatres. Once Wagner understood how tenuous the future of Bayreuth was, he gave permission for complete cycles to be performed elsewhere. This was first done in Leipzig between April and September 1878, followed by complete cycles in Munich in November 1878, Vienna in 1879, and Hamburg in 1880 (*BaRW*, 231). *The Valkyrie*, always the most popular of *The Ring* dramas, was given on its own at several smaller theatres. The person mainly responsible for this spread of Wagner's work was the theatrical entrepreneur, Angelo Neumann, who had first persuaded Wagner to release the rights to the cycle. His production in Leipzig was so successful that he determined to bring it to Berlin. Theatrical politics denied him the Berlin Court Theatre, so he contracted for the commercial Viktoria Theatre where, in May 1881, four performances of the complete cycle were given. Not only was this celebrated event an important moment in Berlin theatre history, but for Wagner it had great personal significance as well. For the first time, he claimed that he had seen one of his own stage pieces as if it were the work of another man, and he was fully satisfied with it. He wrote to Ludwig:

The most extraordinary aspect of it was that this work that has made such severe demands was now entirely new to me. I let it spread out before me in the most complete objectivity, permitting everything to pass by purely and clearly as if reflected in the mirror of my soul, and my judgment was—great satisfaction, mixed with some astonishment, that such a work had been created in our time, and—that it had finally been possible to bring it before an audience in a great city, without evoking their dislike and rejection. (*LuWB*, III, 208)

At last, Wagner seemed to be coming to terms with the realities of theatrical life. His confidence in Neumann led to the producer's taking *The Ring* to London in 1882, right at the time when the city was enjoying its own Wagner Festival at Drury Lane with a season of *Tannhäuser*, *Lohengrin*, *Tristan*, and *The Mastersingers*. Later that year, Neumann formed a company that earned renown touring *The Ring* in Austria, Germany, Italy, and the Netherlands. In 1889, Newmann sponsored productions of *The Ring* in St. Petersburg and Moscow. In fact, due mainly to Neumann's efforts, Wagner enjoyed unaccustomed financial security in the final years of his life.

On the domestic front, life at Wahnfried was serene. When he was not traveling or busy with festival matters, Wagner's time was taken up with the composition of *Parsifal*, with the education of the five children who formed the nucleus of the household (Illustration 12), and with evenings with Cosima reading the classics. A threat to domestic peace came from the French writer, Judith Gautier, daughter of Théophile Gautier and one-time wife of the poet Catulle Mendès, who had first visited Wagner in Tribschen in 1869. She had later attended the first festival, where she and Wagner developed a relationship of considerable intimacy. Probably nothing came of it, although they engaged in a correspondence that suggests that he was strongly attracted to her. This came to a sudden end in Feburary 1878, probably at the insistence of Cosima, who may have discovered it. A further cause for disquiet was Wagner's health. Even as a young man, he had rarely enjoyed the best of health; now it was severely damaged by his prolonged efforts to build the festival. There were increasing signs of a chronic heart condition, though doctors were unwilling to diagnose organic deficiencies. Added to this, Wagner found the dismal Bayreuth climate debilitating. Consequently, he took extended trips to Italy; in addition to the holiday after the first festival, he and the family spent the whole of 1880 and six months of 1881–1882 in the milder Mediterranean climate. That is also where he spent the final months of his life.

Illustration 12. The Wagner family at Wahnfried, 1882. (From left to right: back row, Blandine (Cosima's daughter), philosopher Heinrich von Stein, Cosima, Richard, Paul von Joukowsky (designer of *Parsifal*); front row, Isolde, Daniele (Cosima's daughter), Eva, Siegfried. Reproduced by permission of the Nationalarchiv der Richard-Wagner-Stiftung/Richard-Wagner-Gedenkstätte, Bayreuth.)

One important consequence of the meeting of patrons in 1877 was the foundation of the periodical *Bayreuther Blätter*, which would be devoted exclusively to propagating Wagner's ideas on theatre, art, and other matters. Edited by the young scholar Hans von Wolzogen, the journal became the major outlet for Wagner's prose writings in his last years. Several essays published at this time betray a hardening of his anti-Semitism and an increasing disdain for those of his countrymen who were not prepared to sacrifice to further the Wagnerian cause. He espoused too the causes of anti-vivisection and, without observing it in his personal diet, vegetarianism. Several later writings were about mystical experience and the religious function of art, indicating an intensification in his concept of the religious nature of the festival theatre.

A crucial shift in Wagner's theory of the total work of art can be found in his essay "Beethoven," which had been published back in 1870 when he was still composing *The Ring*. Here he designated a priority in the separate components of tone, word, and physical production, which, in his previous theoretical writings, were equal in importance. Now music, as the unmediated expression both of the Schopenhauerian will and of emotional experience, was accorded priority. Words, Wagner argued, are not necessary to understand the experience that music embodies, for music is a more powerful medium than poetry in setting a mood. Even the visual aspects of drama have more direct impact upon the spectator's mood than words. Hence, a combination of music and spectacle should henceforth be the main aim of his stage work, with poetry in a supportive role. This shift in priorities was not readily apparent in *Twilight of the Gods*, primarily because that drama completed work that had been initiated at a period when Wagner had believed that words were of greater importance, although, even here, purely orchestral passages and the symphonic nature of the orchestra were more evident than in the previous dramas of *The Ring*.

The earliest indication of the preeminence of music above the other elements of performance appears in *Tristan* and becomes fully apparent in Wagner's final work, *Parsifal*. In the "Beethoven" essay, he expressed a newly elevated concept of the musician. Because the musician has such instant access to the most profound aspects of human experience, Wagner asserted that we must "pay [him] more reverence than we do other artists, indeed almost grant him a claim to divine status" (*GSB*, VIII, 156). Perhaps as a consequence of this belief, Wagner came to regard Bayreuth less as a mere theatre and more as a shrine, where the ultimate glory would be the unveiling of *Parsifal*. Bayreuth, he wrote to Ludwig, would be "the pinnacle of all my achievements," and even *The Ring* itself would be regarded as solely a means to an end, which was:

to build a Castle of the Grail for art, far away from the common byways of human undertakings; for only there, in that Monsalvat, can the greatly desired deed be unveiled to the people, to the initiates, and not in a place where God may not reveal Himself before the idols of the day without being blasphemed. (*LuWB*, III, 22)

In her *Diaries*, which provide a day-by-day account of the last fourteen years of Wagner's life, Cosima consistently invested the Bayreuth Festival Theatre with an aura of sanctity. Sometimes she associated it with Christianity, the simplicity of its appointments reminding her of "the crib of our Savior" (*CWD*, II, 357). Sometimes she called upon more exotic religions; once, visiting the still-to-be-completed theatre on a Christmas Day, she described it as "an Assyrian edifice, the pillars ranged like sphinxes below" (CWD, I, 713). Under any circumstances, she insisted on it as a building "dedicated wholly to the sublime" (*CWD*, II, 692).

Aligned with this growing sense of the religious mission of the festival theatre was an intensification in both Wagner's writings and Cosima's *Diaries* of an active dislike of the physicality of theatre. After his newly won acceptance of theatre at the Berlin *Ring*, Wagner started to suspect it once again. For example, in a sentiment that would have won the approval if not the credulity of Nietzsche, Wagner wished he were only a literary writer so that he need not pander to theatre audiences, the "most grotesque section of the public" (*CWD*, I, 510), and he indignantly rejected the idea that his son Siegfried might become a play actor (*CWD*, I, 739). But what is most notable in Wagner's continuing ruminations was his growing suspicion that theatre was, by its very nature, an impossible medium for his art. For most of his life, however much he inveighed against the inadequacies of the contemporary theatre, he had assumed that in order for his music to be understood fully, it needed stage representation. But with *Parsifal* he thought differently. "Costumes and greasepaint," he averred, in a rejection of those visual properties of theatre that he had affirmed in "Beethoven," would violate the imaginative realms evoked by the music. Instead, he commented wryly, "having created the invisible orchestra, I now feel like inventing the invisible theatre" (*CWD*, II, 154). Complaints such as these became more frequent after the production of *The Ring*, because the ideal perspective and closeness provided by the Festival Theatre had intensified Wagner's awareness of the inadequacies of his production, until he reached the point of doubting the viability of producing *Parsifal* at all. Ultimately, one suspects, he would have preferred not to see it staged. Indeed, while writing it, the only theatrical activities that seemed to offer him any satisfaction were private readings of great world drama or of his own works that he gave most frequently to the smallest and most accepting audience of all, Cosima. "Splendid, blessed hours," she called these readings, "such as no public performance could ever provide" (*CWD*, II, 30).

Nevertheless, despite his doubts, *Parsifal* was given its first performance at the Bayreuth Festival Theatre on 26 July 1882. In Wagner's mind, this was no ordinary theatrical occurrence. Instead, performance of this "Stage-Dedication Festival Play," as he labeled it, consummated the quasi-religious function that he considered Bayreuth to serve. *Parsifal* he regarded as the culmination of his creative life. In fact, no work, not even *The Ring*, had occupied his imagination for such an extended stretch of time. His interest in the myth of Parsifal had first arisen back in 1845 when he read the medieval poet Wolfram von Eschenbach's epic *Parzifal*. Later, when drafting *Tristan*, he had considered introducing Parzifal into act 3, an idea he abandoned as it was not intrinsic to the action. Then, in 1857, the day after moving into the "Asyl" on the Wesendonk property in Zürich, Wagner experienced a feeling of serenity and oneness with nature that he identified with the atmosphere of Good Friday, leading him to write a preliminary sketch for *Parsifal*. Eight years later, in August 1865, at the request of Ludwig, he wrote an extended prose scenario upon which the final work would be based. It was not until *The Ring* had finally been performed at Bayreuth, however, that he found the peace of mind to concentrate on what he knew would be his last major composition. He set to work on the poem soon after returning from his post-*Ring* holiday in Italy and finished it in April 1877. In August of the same year, he began composition, finishing the orchestral sketch by April 1879. The full score was not completed until January 1882, while he was staying in Palermo. Ill health had considerably delayed its completion.

Parsifal is set in Monsalvat, the castle of the Grail in the mountains of northern Spain, and in the castle of Klingsor on the southern slopes of the same mountain range. Amfortas, the King of the Grail, is plagued by a spear wound that he received from Klingsor at the moment when he was being seduced by a "fearfully beautiful woman." The wound will not heal and is reopened each time Amfortas, in his duty as king, reveals the Grail to his knights. From a vision, he has learnt that a cure will come only when he is visited by a "pure fool, enlightened by compassion." The action begins when Parsifal, an innocent child of nature, shoots a wild swan on the grounds of Monsalvat. He is brought by the knights before Gurnemanz, who, after reproving him for the killing, conducts him to the castle. There he observes, uncomprehendingly, the ritual of the Grail and the reopening of Amfortas' wound. Gurnemanz turns Parsifal out of the castle. In act 2,

Parsifal encounters Kundry, who has already appeared as a servant of the Knights of the Grail but is now a slave of Klingsor. Klingsor hopes to enslave Parsifal by having Kundry seduce him, but Parsifal resists Kundry, after her kiss awakens within him compassion rather than sexual desire. Klingsor attempts to wound Parsifal with the spear, but it miraculously stops above the youth's head and Parsifal departs carrying the spear. After several years, Parsifal returns to Monsalvat on a serene Good Friday. He learns that the knighthood is failing because Amfortas no longer reveals the Grail to them. He, the "pure fool, enlightened by compassion," now reenters the castle, touches Amfortas' wound with the spear, and heals it. The final ritual enthrones Parsifal as the new King of the Grail.

None of Wagner's works has aroused as much controversy as *Parsifal*. When it was first performed, several felt that it represented a decline in his powers as a dramatist and composer, while others saw it as the summit of his achievement. A similar division of opinion exists today. Certainly, it is more difficult to come to terms with than the earlier works. It is similar to *Tristan* in that much of the action is metaphorical for the experience of the central character, except that while the sensuous music of *Tristan* is emotionally gripping, that of *Parsifal* is serene and refined. The action is not entirely lacking in incident, but the work is not crammed with events like *The Ring*. In act 2, for example, Parsifal battles offstage with the knights guarding Klingsor's castle; later the castle is transformed into an exotic garden, and, at the end, there is the incident with the spear and the transformation of the garden into a desert. But these spectacular events are not realized in the music as they would have been earlier in Wagner's career. Rather, the music, which, in Liszt's words, moves from "the sublime to the ultra-sublime"[2] is dedicated primarily to evoking a metaphysical realm that lies beyond the plane of purely human action.

The serenity of *Parsifal* causes a distinct lack of dramatic momentum. The poem is one of the shortest that Wagner ever wrote, even though the musical work, depending on the individual conductor's pace, is usually one of the longest to perform. In acts 1 and 3 especially, words are delivered at a uniformly slow pace, and the exposition has a static quality more suited to the epic than the drama. The whole of act 3 unfolds a process that is easily foreseen and involves no conflict. Important passages that would once have been sung are now left to the orchestra. In particular, the famous transformation passages in acts 1 and 3, when Gurnemanz leads Parsifal to the castle, are purely scenic and orchestral, but, in the course of them, Parsifal's knowledge of himself and the world is greatly expanded. Only in act 2 are the rhythms faster and more varied. Here

Kundry's exposition, in which she tells Parsifal about his parents, his childhood, and his mother's death, has a fully dramatic function as it contributes to Parsifal's growth.

The undramatic quality of *Parsifal* is underlined by the manner in which he grows. Parsifal, a pure child of nature, is initially similar to Siegfried, but he matures antithetically to the earlier hero. On the verge of being overcome by the regressive world of the senses that is represented by Kundry and, by association, his mother, he learns compassion and the suffering this entails. He achieves self-knowledge not through indulging the senses but by overcoming them. Nevertheless, he is no passive hero. His compassion has a positive effect on others, as it impels them to unity and away from division. Conflict is neutralized through Parsifal, and his compassion ultimately embraces all in its lyrical vision.

Parsifal demonstrates no falling off in Wagner's powers of dramaturgy, which are as economical as ever. For example, his source material, primarily Eschenbach's epic, has Parsifal perpetuate the sufferings of the Amfortas figure because he fails to ask a question on the meaning of the ritual. Wagner avoids this trivial issue by combining the myth of the Grail with that of the spear that pierced Christ's side and that Klingsor has plundered from Amfortas. In Klingsor's hands, it is a weapon of destruction, but the moment that it passes to Parsifal, it becomes an instrument of healing. We do not see the process by which this comes about. The spear simply changes into a symbol of the spiritual power of Parsifal's personality.

Kundry is commonly regarded as Wagner's most complex character, possibly because in her he disregards the conventions of dramatic characterization whereby character is a comparatively fixed combination of symbolic and individual elements. Kundry is entirely symbolic, functioning only as required by the pattern of the work. Hence, in act 1, she is an abject and surly presence; in act 2, an alluring seducer; in act 3, again an abject slave and then a beautific convert. Essentially, she stands for the forces of the natural world that can either obstruct or facilitate the movement of humanity toward salvation.

In contrast with previous works, there are comparatively few leitmotifs, and these are both difficult to distinguish and almost impossible to identify with dramatic themes, characters, or aspects of the action. The sameness of much of the music has been seen as evidence of Wagner's declining powers. Nevertheless, in a finely judged performance, the unchanging nature of the music guides one's sensibilities toward an awareness of eternal values that lie beyond the Grail, values that clearly have precedence over purely human ones.

Perhaps the main reason for the offense *Parsifal* was and is still capable of causing lies in Wagner's seeming use of theatre for religious purposes. While it may be difficult to agree with its most articulate defender, who sees the work as a dramatization of "the psychopathology of religious belief" (*TWC*, 209), it is undoubtedly about religious experience. It does not require the audience to behave as if participating in a ritual, although audiences' consistent refusal to clap after act 1, a custon not sanctioned by Wagner, suggests they might wish to do so. Moreover, one does not have to be a Christian to appreciate *Parsifal* or to find its action credible; in the Grail scenes, Wagner used sections of the Christian mass but did not recreate it. Indeed, the philosophical aura of the work owes as much to Schopenhauer and Buddha as it does to Christianity. To appreciate the drama fully, however, one must concur with its premise that human and metaphyusical realms are capable of exercising a tangible influence on each other. In other words, *Parsifal* requires an act of belief whereas other of Wagner's works do not. While the vision of transfigured nature summoned up by the Good Friday music is an experience that most audiences can recognize, the action implies a religious presence. Nietzsche may have been wrong in his specific diagnosis of Wagner's Christianity, but he still could not accept the spiritual atmosphere of *Parsifal*.

Despite Wagner's doubts as to the suitability of *Parsifal* for performance, in the intense environment of the Festival Theatre, it was remarkably successful. Paul von Joukowsky's sets, especially the Temple of the Grail (see the set in Illustration 9), based upon Siena Cathedral, provided an apt setting for the elevated action within the realistic conventions of the time. The transformations of acts 1 and 3 were achieved by a panorama mounted on rollers, which changed in coordination with the music. Technical problems led to the transformation of act 3 having to take place with the curtain drawn, but the act 1 passage was effective, a practical demonstration of the principles of the "Beethoven" essay. But, if the Viennese critic Hanslick is anything to go by, the more reassuringly human action of act 2 and the sensuous flower maidens that first tempt Parsifal to indulgence were the most appealing aspect of the performance.[3] Wagner, despite his reservations about the whole question of production, was generally happy with the results. His report on the performances in fact suggests that he was searching for a new mode of stage representation suited for his abstract material. He required from his intensely rehearsed singers absolute clarity in rendition and a "conscientious moderation" in movement (*GSB*, II, 372). Half rather than full gestures were encouraged. He insisted that simplicity was the essence of the staging, with no realistic action or the "false pathos" of conventional operatic acting. The main roles were also doubly or triply cast so that, over one month, sixteen performances with alternating casts could be given, with the quality of singing and acting noticeably improving in the course of the run. For the first time in his life, Wagner had achieved theatrical conditions he considered ideal. To crown it all, this was the first and last of his projects to earn a considerable profit.

Wagner knew that *Parsifal* was to be his last work. Anything he wrote had to have a gestation period of several years before he was ready to compose it, and he had no further projects in mind. If he was to continue composing, he claimed, it would be in the field of purely instrumental music.

He left Bayreuth on 6 September 1882 for a prolonged stay in Italy. A few days later, he and his family settled into an eighteen-room wing of the Vendramin Palace in Venice. Here he received several visitors, especially Liszt, who stayed a month. Initially there was no sign of an imminent decline in his health. As irascible and impulsive as ever, he was given to exuberant outbursts characteristic of a person a third of his age. He even engaged in a little conducting, rehearsing the orchestra of the Liceo Marcello in the symphony that he had composed fifty years earlier. The performance, which was private, occurred on 25 December in honor of Cosima's birthday. Gradually, however, the heart cramps that had tormented him for the previous four or five years returned and increased in frequency. On 13 February 1883, while seated at his desk and working on an article "On the Womanly," he suffered a fatal heart attack.

The ceremony that accompanied the return of Wagner's body to Bayreuth revealed the fame he had achieved. The coffin, closely attended by the deeply grieving Cosima, traveled in a special train. At the German border, it was met by a representative of King Ludwig, and, in Munich, a public ceremony of mourning took place at the railway station. Finally, at Bayreuth, an elaborate funeral procession carried the body back to Wahnfried, where it was buried in a mausoleum in the garden. It would be another forty-seven years before Cosima joined her husband there.

NOTES

1. Friedrich Nietzsche, *Human, All Too Human*, trans. R. J. Hollingdale (Cambridge: Cambridge University Press, 1986), 88.

2. Lucy Beckett, *Richard Wagner: Parsifal* (Cambridge: Cambridge University Press, 1981), 103–105.

3. Robert Hartford, ed., *Bayreuth: The Early Years* (Cambridge: Cambridge University Press, 1980), 125 (henceforward *HBEY*).

Chapter 9

Wagner's Theatrical Legacy

[Your music] possesses greatness, and it makes one experience
greatness. I have encountered everywhere in your works the solemnity of the great sounds, the great aspects of nature, and the
solemnity of the great passions of man. One feels himself immediately carried away and subjugated. . . . I felt all the majesty of a life
that is more ample than our own. . . . Throughout, there is something exalted and exalting, something aspiring to mount higher,
something excessive.[1]

These words, written by Charles Baudelaire to Wagner after the French
poet had heard one of the 1860 concerts in Paris, describe accurately the
paradoxical appeal of Wagner's work. Like most successful opera, it
exhilarates, leading us perhaps "to think ourselves greater than we are."[2]
At the same time, as those who have sat through an uncut performance of
Twilight of the Gods may testify, Wagner's music can also leave one with
the strangely morbid feeling of having been buried beneath a mountain of
sound. Wagner excites and exhausts to greater extremes than any other
classic composer or dramatist. No doubt this is partially the reason for the
fascination that his work has consistently exercised on subsequent generations. Given the growing popularity of opera in contemporary Europe and
America, there is no sign, over one hundred years after his death, that this
fascination is abating.

Few artists in turn-of-the-century Europe, regardless of the medium in
which they worked, could escape his influence. Giacomo Puccini, who

studied his work endlessly, hit the right note of despair when he flung the score of *Tristan* from him, exclaiming "Enough of this music! We're mandolinists, amateurs; woe to him who gets caught by it! This tremendous music destroys one and renders one incapable of composing any more!"[3] Richard Strauss, the leading opera composer of the next generation, never escaped Wagner's influence, either in his orchestral color or his use of the leitmotif, which he applied even more systematically than its progenitor did.

Literary writers found him equally seductive. An exhaustive survey of Wagner's influence on literature has demonstrated that he was a major source of inspiration for novelists as different as Marcel Proust, Thomas Mann, Virginia Woolf, and D. H. Lawrence, one of them in particular—Mann—spending his whole life coming to terms with the impact of Wagner upon his personal creativity and the life of twentieth-century Germany.[4] Wagner served French composers and *literati* mainly as an inspiration for their own decadent art, as expounded in the pages of *La revue Wagnerienne*, a periodical whose view of Wagner as a neurasthenic aesthete would hardly have met with his approval.

Wagner's impact upon the theatre cannot be overexaggerated. Many important fin-de-siècle playwrights clearly came under his spell. Strindberg's later plays, particularly *A Dream Play* and the "Chamber Plays," employ the leitmotif as a major structural principle, a practice that can also be traced in other playwrights of a symbolist bent. But Wagner's impact upon the institution of theatre has been still more pronounced and consequential. The Bayreuth Festival has provided Europe with a paradigm that it has since found extraordinarily congenial. Indeed, only a year after the first performance of *The Ring*, Richter conducted the Vienna Philharmonic Orchestra in three concerts of Mozart's music in Salzburg; from this grew the idea of a festival in Salzburg devoted to its most distinguished son. When the Salzburg Festival was eventually established in 1920, the repertoire was not confined to Mozart, and orchestral music as well as spoken theatre became as prominent as opera. Nevertheless, despite many differences, Salzburg also embodied the Wagnerian ideal of a festival as a sanctuary of art, far removed from the pollution of a modern, industrial civilization.[5] The influence of Bayreuth was pervasive. While the opera festival at Glyndebourne in the southern English countryside is known for championing Mozart, its founder, John Christie was a habitué of Bayreuth, and the first music ever to be performed at Glyndebourne, in June 1928, was in fact act 3, scene 1, of *The Mastersingers*.[6]

Bayreuth had had its impact on the spoken theatre as well. The foundation stone of the Shakespeare Memorial Theatre at Stratford-upon-Avon in England was laid only nine months after the opening of the Bayreuth Festival, and, over the years of struggle to found a permanent festival there, the model of Bayreuth was constantly evoked.[7] Meanwhile, of all the influences inspiring W. B. Yeats during the foundation of the Irish National Theatre, which eventually became the Abbey Theatre, Wagner's Bayreuth Festival was probably the most powerful.[8] The appetite for arts festivals seems never to be satisfied. The second half of the twentieth century in particular has seen a proliferation of music and theatre festivals. Now those who have sufficient leisure and money can spend a whole summer attending festival performances in cities where they enjoy monuments of historical interest and scenic beauty in the day and exemplary performances of music and theatre in the evening. Indeed, the ideal of a festival as a temporary utopia of art removed from the stressful life of the big city is more alive today than at any time during or since the late nineteenth century.

The actual theatre at Bayreuth has also been widely imitated. Its auditorium probably provided Strindberg with the model theatre that he envisioned in his "Preface to *Miss Julie*." The present Shakespeare Theatre in Stratford was initially modeled on Bayreuth; in fact, so ubiquitous has the prototypical form of a single bank of seats in a wedge or fan shape become that, in America, it is frequently referred to as the "European" auditorium. Although the horseshoe auditorium of the Italian opera house is still perhaps the dominant prototype for the modern opera house (on those rare occasions when such a building is erected), the configuration of Bayreuth is considered most suitable for the spoken theatre, no doubt because of its ideal sightlines and the degree of concentration it encourages among spectators, a concentration difficult to achieve in auditoria where the audience is divided into stalls, balconies, and galleries.

The reforms that Wagner envisaged in the organization of the repertoire have also been widely adopted. While it would be unrealistic to claim that proposals such as those contained in the 1848 Plan to reorganize the Saxon theatre or in the 1851 essay "A Theatre in Zürich" have directly influenced changing patterns of repertoire, the modern theatre is organized in a structure closer to that envisaged by Wagner. In Germany especially, generous subsidies have allowed for the creation of permanent companies of actors and singers who are not as overworked as they were in Wagner's time, while a considerable expansion of the theatre-going population over the last hundred years has led to a substantial decline in the number of separate productions each theatre must give. Now adequate rehearsal time and frequent repetitions of a production mean that theatre need not automatically fall into the stale and automatic routines that Wagner deplored. Although the German theatre is far from a paradise—opera companies, for example, can still be afflicted by the star syndrome—in structure and in ties to the community, theatres in general are closer to the model Wagner imagined.

But his main legacy to the modern theatre continues to be his music dramas, which remain central to the repertoire. Indeed, they have acquired a canonical status over which Wagner, a professed enemy of stasis and monumentalism, might have felt uneasy. In fact, there was little danger that his works would be forgotten after his death. Few artists in any medium have had such an apparatus devoted to perpetuating their fame as he did. Before his death, he gave no indication as to who should assume the immediate direction of the festival; his son Siegfried was expected eventually to take over. Cosima, however, had no doubts that she was the one to guarantee the survival of her husband's work. Taking imperious control of the festival, she began by reviving *Parsifal* only a few months after Wagner's death. Over the next several years, she staged all those works that he considered to comprise his unique contribution to the development of music and the theatre. Thus, by 1901, all his music dramas from *The Flying Dutchman* on had been produced on the Bayreuth stage. The Bayreuth Festival remains to this day an annual festival devoted exclusively to the production of these ten works. Protests have been made that such a repertoire is too narrow and that Wagner intended at least Mozart, Beethoven, and Weber to be played at Bayreuth as well, but his works still form the sole repertoire.

Cosima proceeded out of reverence, her purpose being to stage the music dramas in precisely the way that Wagner had intended. Hence, the productions of *Tristan and Isolde* and *The Mastersingers* (first staged at Bayreuth in 1886 and 1888 respectively) were scrupulously based on whatever documentation remained of the first productions in Munich. *Tannhäuser*, first produced in the Festival Theatre in 1891, was expertly put together from the various versions that had been given in Dresden, Paris, and Vienna. The dominant style of the productions was the historicist romantic-realism in which Wagner had originally conceived all his dramas. Cosima never hesitated to engage art historians and archaeologists to ensure the historical authenticity of costumes and settings. In doing this, she ignored indications that, toward the end of his life, Wagner himself was coming to doubt the efficacy of a predominantly realistic approach. But he had no clear alternatives to offer, so the most fitting memorials to his work were productions that followed as closely as possible his stage directions and directorial practice. Bayreuth in its early years was primarily a museum theatre.

There is one way in which Cosima differed significantly from her husband. She was an excellent businesswoman. Under her management, the Bayreuth Festival achieved solvency and early in the twentieth century even began to show a healthy profit. She achieved this in part by limiting the performance of his music dramas elsewhere (*Parsifal*, for example, in obedience to Wagner's wishes, was not produced outside Bayreuth until 1913, except for some performances at the Metropolitan Opera in New York), in part by sound economics, and in part by canny showmanship. She successfully created the image of Bayreuth as the fount of wisdom in all matters Wagnerian, so that annual August pilgrimages to Bayreuth became a regular event in the calendar of well-heeled opera lovers. Indeed, attendance at the Festival Theatre was an act akin to worshipping at a shrine, as Mark Twain, with little sense of irony, reported after seeing *Tristan and Isolde* in 1891. It was "one of the most extraordinary experiences of my life," he wrote. "I have never seen anything like this before. I have never seen anything so great and fine and real as this devotion" (*HBEY*, 155). Countless eyewitness narratives confirm Twain's account.

Siegfried Wagner eventually took over as director of the festival in 1908. A man of more than modest talents, he was a composer in his own right, an effective conductor, and a stage director whose work was at times compared, not unfavorably, to that of Max Reinhardt. Nevertheless, inhibited perhaps by the intimidating presence of his mother, who died only a few months before he did in 1930, he did little to alter the basic conception of staging at Bayreuth. Kurt Söhnlein's sets for Siegfried's 1927 production of *Tristan and Isolde* were considerably more abstract than the ones Cosima had employed, as were the sets for the 1930 production of *Tannhäuser*, but Siegfried died before any radical move away from Bayreuth realism could be made.

The infiltration of abstract settings onto the Bayreuth stage may well have been due, indirectly, to the influence of Adolphe Appia. When the young Swiss stage designer attended *Parsifal* in 1882 and *Tristan and Isolde* and *The Mastersingers* in 1888, he was deeply disappointed by his perception of a conflict between the stage and the music. He found the expansive, suggestive influence of the music to be deadened by the prosaic sets. The consequent revolution in scenic design effected by Appia arose primarily from his desire to see Wagner's music dramas given as complete a production as possible, in which settings, staging, and acting would complement perfectly the imaginative world suggested by the music.

Appia set out his ideas on the staging of Wagner in two books *La Mise en scène du drame Wagnérien* (*The Production of Wagnerian Drama*) and *La Musique et la mise en scène* (*Music and Production*), published in 1895 and 1899 respectively. In them, he argued that Wagnerian drama produced a life of its own, in which duration was determined solely by the music, not by any approximation of time as experienced in everyday life. By the same token, stage space had no relation to space outside the theatre, for it was used solely to embody the imaginative world conjured up by the music. Music, Appia argued, was the sole force that could combine all elements of production and performance and should therefore determine all aspects of design, staging, and enactment. Essentially, Appia challenged the theoretical equality of all theatrical elements as expounded in the essays that Wagner wrote between 1849 and 1851, which define the total work of art. Instead, he adopted a position closer to that outlined in "Beethoven," which established a hierarchy of elements in which music was preeminent. The sets, which were published as illustrations to Appia's book, were highly stylized, abstract, and devised to intensify the suggestiveness of the music, not to distract from it by focusing on realistic details. Light rather than paint would be the main purveyor of color, since the flexibility with which light could change both in intensity and color provided an effective analog to shifts of mood in the music. The singing-actor, for whom the set must provide an acceptable environment, should engage in movement and gesture only to the extent required by the music.

Despite the seeming novelty of his ideas and set designs, Appia was working in the spirit of "total theatre" as envisaged by Wagner, in that all the elements involved in the performance of music drama had to work in total harmony with each other. The stage production was to be a seamless, organic whole, in which each element complemented the others, but also so that the music received the fullest possible realization. Cosima, however, saw no connection between Appia's ideas and those of her husband. When Appia presented his ideas to her, she dismissed them in her characteristically emphatic manner, claiming that Wagner had fixed the staging of his music dramas for all time. Nonetheless, even Cosima was not immune to the tendency of the time to simplify. Over the years, her production of *Tristan and Isolde*, though based on the original Munich production, underwent much modification in costuming, a progressive reduction in pomp, and a considerable simplification in gesture, all of which brought the performance closer to the "spiritual chamberplay" she understood the drama to be. Even so, she never countenanced a reformulation as drastic as that envisaged by Appia.

Appia was a theorist rather than a practitioner, and his own productions, of Wagner or anyone else, were few and far between. The first Wagnerian drama he staged was *Tristan and Isolde* at La Scala in Milan, at the invitation of Arturo Toscanini, in 1923. The production was not a popular success. The sets were severely abstract rather than illusionist and lacked the conventional romantic atmosphere that audiences associated with the work. Critical reception was mixed; only some writers recognized the aptness of Appia's use of darkness and dim light as stage metaphors for the lovers' desire to retreat from the world into utter self-absorption.[9] Despite the unusual beauty of Appia's work, the production soon disappeared to be replaced by a more conventional one that perpetuated the staging habits of the nineteenth century. Soon after the La Scala production, Appia was commissioned to direct *The Ring* at the Basel City Opera, in cooperation with the stage director Oskar Wälterlin. The cubistic sets he designed lacked the poetry of his earlier designs for *The Ring*, as published in his books on the staging of Wagner, and they clashed strangely with the traditional costumes of winged helmets, heavy skirts, and breastplates. Since Appia's ideas were by now making some headway in Germany, however, audiences did not find his scenic ideas too difficult to stomach, and it looked as though the productions were on the way to being a success. But a group of conservatives who still considered Bayreuth the last word in staging Wagner's work protested so vigorously that Appia and Wälterlin had to abandon the project halfway through; *Siegfried* and *Twilight of the Gods* remained unproduced. Appia died in obscurity a few years later.

While Appia's ideas were seminal in the modern production of Wagner, his productions were not the first to challenge the traditional approach of Bayreuth. For example, in 1903, *Tristan and Isolde* was given a celebrated production at the Vienna State Opera, conducted by Gustav Mahler and designed by Alfred Roller in the style of the Vienna Secession (*BaRW*, 150). Though Roller did not entirely eschew realism, his use of light and atmospheric detail to materialize the emotions of the lovers was fully in accord with Appia's ideas. So too was Vsevolod Meyerhold's production of the same opera at the Maryinsky Theatre in St. Petersburg in 1909, in which historicist detail was abandoned in order to maintain a complete atmosphere of "fairy-tale" (*BaRW*, 151). In the late 1920s and early 1930s, Jürgen Fehling and Otto Klemperer were responsible for productions of *The Flying Dutchman* and *Tannhäuser* in the unromantic manner of *neue Sachlichkeit* or "new objectivity."

The dissemination of Appia's ideas through the German theatre was facilitated by the vogue for expressionist drama, for his basic conception of theatre space had much in common with expressionism. By the 1930s, not even Bayreuth could escape entirely the tendency toward abstract design. Under the artistic direction of the Berlin conductor and stage director Heinz Tietjen, both *The Ring*, with sets by Emil Preetorius, and

Parsifal, with sets by Alfred Roller, were staged largely free of historicist detail in a style clearly influenced by Appia. Political circumstances, however, prevented Bayreuth from developing into a center of artistic experimentation. The close friendship between Adolf Hitler and Siegfried Wagner's widow Winifred, who was general manager of the festival during the 1930s, led to the period of Nazi patronage, a state of affairs that Tietjen did not seem to find at all disagreeable. Hence, productions during the late 1930s continued to perpetuate, in slightly modified form, the uncomplicated mode of romantic realism, with the stage serving as a means to display, rather than to express, the music.

The Bayreuth Festival was closed for some years after the Second World War. When it reopened in 1951, under the direction of the composer's grandsons, Wieland and Wolfgang Wagner, it at once became a center for theatrical experimentation, with Appia openly acknowledged as the guiding light of the renovated theatrical enterprise. The first postwar festival included new productions of *Parsifal*, *The Ring*, and *The Mastersingers*, all but the last in strikingly minimalist productions without a vestige of realistic representation. Most successful was *Parsifal* in which the strong contrast of light and dark, played out against vague towering forms suggestive of the pillars of the temple or trees in the forest (Illustration 13), embodied the fluctuations of Parsifal's consciousness and realized, perhaps for the first time, the inner action of Wagner's work. "We felt the forest rather than saw it," wrote Ernest Newman, "a legendary forest that was of no time and no place and one, moreover, over which mystery and sorrow and pain seemed to have brooded long."[10]

In the course of the next two decades, the entire canon was reworked in the minimalist style that became the hallmark of the Wagner grandsons. The music dramas were staged with the focus on the mythical action and virtually no concern for historical or local atmosphere in setting and costumes. Scenery was designed to release rather than inhibit the audience's imagination, intensifying their response to the music. Stage action was also minimal, so that a production like Wieland's *Lohengrin* (1958–1960) appeared more an oratorio in costume than a fully staged music drama. Some productions were among the landmark events in the history of the modern theatre, such as Wieland's *Tristan and Isolde* (1962–1971), staged with towering scenic units based on elemental Celtic forms. These absorbed the deeply erotic tones of the action, while the unusually flexible lighting conveyed the slightest change in the dynamics of the lovers' feelings and embodied the dominant metaphor of light and dark. Even *The Mastersingers*, of all Wagner's works the one that would seem most impervious to such treatment, set as it is in so specific a time

Illustration 13. Act 3 of *Parsifal*, directed and designed by Wieland Wagner, Bayreuth, 1951. (With Jerome Hines as Gurnemanz, Hans Beirer as Parsifal and Regine Crespin as Kundry. Reproduced by permission of Bayreuther Festspiele GmbH/Foto Lauterwasser.)

and place, was staged in a spare poetic style in which references to sixteenth-century Nuremberg were reduced to a minimum (1956–1961). Later (1963–1964), it was restaged in a neo-Brechtian mode, on a permanent wooden set based on an Elizabethan theatre; this production emphasized the venality and fallibility of Nuremberg society.

These "new Bayreuth" productions were initially received with hostility, since they flagrantly ignored Wagner's original stage directions and eschewed the realistic spectacle that had, despite some changes, been standard until the Second World War. They were ultimately accepted, however, due in part to the beauty and aptness of the staging; indeed, Wieland's spare style has had a major impact upon the production of opera worldwide. But perhaps the main reason why "new Bayreuth" came eventually to be accepted was that it extended rather than denied the basic concept of "total theatre." It retained an "organic" approach, in which each element complemented every other, and so the seamless unity of all theatrical components remained central to the productions' appeal. Although the Wagners' approach to characterization was novel and difficult to accept—in particular, they divested the figures of *The Ring* of their customary heroic stature—aesthetically they remained within the pale of theatre as originally conceived by their grandfather.

Recently, there have been fundamental changes in the approach to Wagner. These have occurred as part of a larger shift within theatre as a whole, both in Germany and internationally, and in both music theatre and spoken theatre. That shift has transferred the center of artistic interest from the musical or spoken text of a stage work to the staging by which the text is realized. In other words, the director rather than the composer/dramatist has increasingly become the central figure of the artistic event, and the production itself is of as much or even more interest than the performance of the music. Ideally, even in the productions of "new Bayreuth," the director aspired ultimately to be an invisible presence, concerned with releasing the latent meanings of the action and unfolding the multiple layers of feeling within the music. A new philosophy of directing, of which audiences first became aware perhaps early in the 1970s, has given the director a more polemical position as his artistic vision is emphasized, even at the expense of the work being staged. Not surprisingly, a key site for the intense critical debate caused by this shift of emphasis has centered on productions of Wagner, for the unusual power and individuality of the musical and verbal text make the stage director's exploitation of the work for different ends seem that much more flagrant a descreation.

The main consequence of the rise of what may be called the "postmodernist" director has been a rejection of Wagner's concept of "total theatre."

Ulrich Melchinger, who produced *The Ring* in Cassel between 1970 and 1974, deliberately rejected the "new Bayreuth" style of "unification, harmonization, [in order] wherever necessary to show the fractures."[11] The contradictions and conflicts of Wagner's dramatic action were now to be realized through an equally contradictory and conflicted approach to production. Poetry, tone, movement, and elements of design were used to subvert rather than support each other. Increasingly, staging often confutes the power of the music, anachronisms in design may disrupt the sensitivities of the audience, and passages of action can be presented in a way that overtly violates Wagner's manifest intent.

At its worst, such direction can be pure sensationalism, nothing more than the exhibition of poorly thought out and bizarre ideas that have little if any coherence. At its best, it can product exhilarating theatre that reaffirms rather than denies the greatness of the works staged. Melchinger's production of *The Ring* at Cassel confused audiences with its puzzling mélange of images from various mythological times, from the nineteenth century, the Nazi period, the present day, and a science-fiction future, but later productions in this manner were more coherent. Utilizing concrete but unromantic settings, productions of *The Ring* by Joachim Herz in Leipzig (1973–1976), by Götz Friedrich in London (1974–1976), and most notably by Patrice Chéreau on the occasion of the centenary at Bayreuth in 1976 (Illustration 14), have emphasized the political and economic aspects of the action, bringing to the fore the concerns of Wagner the nineteenth-century revolutionary rather than the romantic mythologist. The riots that greeted the first series of performances of Chéreau's *Ring* at Bayreuth are legendary, but so too is the immense following that this production, admittedly in revised form, had acquired by the time it was withdrawn in 1981. The television version, filmed on the actual stage of Bayreuth, has introduced Wagner to wider audiences than all stage productions since the composer's lifetime. This "postmodern" Wagner is, therefore, for good or ill, the one most widely known.

On the whole, the change has been for the good. Despite the bizarre nature of much contemporary Wagner production, an intelligent stage interpretation can deepen considerably our understanding of the work and its wider cultural import. Hence, *The Flying Dutchman* is now often staged in costumes and settings that are more closely associated with Ibsenesque realism than with romantic mythology. The central action can sometimes be seen from a strikingly unfamiliar viewpoint. Harry Kupfer's controversial and compelling production at Bayreuth in 1978 took Senta rather than the Dutchman as the central character, making the action a fantasy of her schizophrenic personality. Jean Pierre Ponnelle's production of the same

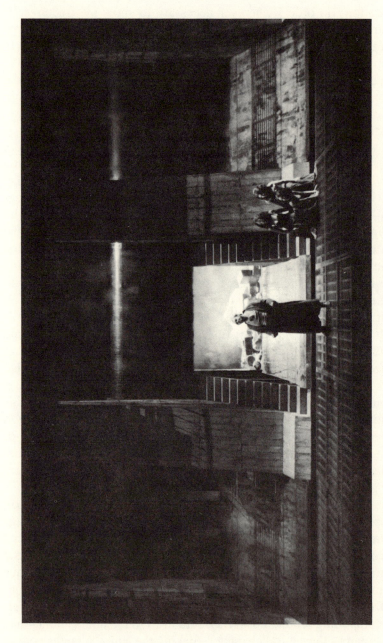

Illustration 14. Scene 1 of *The Rhinegold*, directed by Patrice Chéreau, Bayreuth, 1976. (Designed by Richard Peduzzi, with Hermann Becht as Alberich. Reproduced by permission of Bayreuther Festspiele GmbH/Foto Rauh.)

opera, seen first in San Francisco and then in Chicago and New York, treated the action, often to the ire of audiences, as a dream of the Steersman. Elsa in *Lohengrin*, a more sympathetic and interesting figure than the eponymous hero of that opera, has also been represented as the central character, the action becoming a dream that projects her suppressed sexual desires.

Frequently, a postmodern production of Wagner is as much a commentary upon the work as a representation of it. This can take the form of highlighting autobiographical aspects of the drama. There have been several productions of *Tristan and Isolde* set in a nineteenth-century boudoir, with parallels drawn between Tristan and Wagner, Isolde and Mathilde, and King Mark and Otto Wesendonk, notably by Kupfer in Dresden in 1975 and by the Russian director Yuri Lyubimov in Bologna in 1983. The political uses of Wagner have also been of interest to directors, most obviously the exploitation of Wagner by the Nazis. Recent celebrated productions of *The Ring* by Nikolaus Lehnhoff in Munich in 1987 and by Herbert Wernicke in Brussels in 1991 were set partially in environments created from the iconography of European imperialism and Nazi dictatorship.

Perhaps the main impact of the postmodern revolution in staging Wagner has been the shattering of any uniform approach. While romantic realism was the dominant idiom in Wagner production until the First World War and the minimalism of Wieland and Wolfgang Wagner predominated during the 1950s and 1960s, the contemporary theatre is marked by extreme eclecticism. The early days of Wagnerian production have been recalled in a romantic staging of *The Ring* at the Metropolitan Opera in the mid-1980s and in an acclaimed Ring by the Scottish Opera, currently in production, which borrows from expressionistic modes. Simultaneously, the minimalism of Wagner's grandsons can still be seen, most notably in productions at Bayreuth by Wolfgang Wagner himself.

On a recent two-week visit to Germany, I saw a cross-section of productions that exemplified the variety of ways in which Wagner is staged today. *The Flying Dutchman* at the Deutsches Oper in Berlin and *The Mastersingers of Nuremberg* in Leipzig, while designed and staged in a confrontational manner that required considerable stylization and selection of scenic elements, offered little that was designed specifically to shock or alter the spectator's point of view. Most memorable were the existential despair of the Dutchman, the dark settings that complemented it, and the occasional picturesque staging of the various choruses. The performance of *The Mastersingers* left me filled, as Wagner no doubt intended one should be, with the warmth of the music and spectacle, and renewed in my confidence in the power of art as a regenerative force in society. In Hamburg, the American stage director Robert Wilson had just produced *Parsifal* in a strangely mannered production lacking entirely the props and pictorial spectacle that Wagner had imagined. While this caused a decrease in theatrical excitement—even the spear was mimed—and no little difficulty in following the plot, the few concrete images that Wilson allowed on his stage, especially a bright circle of actual flame for the grail, were imprinted indelibly on the memory. In Wilson, the spare poetry of Wieland Wagner survives.

More controversial was a production in Frankfurt of *Lohengrin* by Lehnhoff. This is the most nationalistic of Wagner's operas, or, at least in its depiction of the Saxons inflamed by the vision of invading hordes from the east, the one most subject to exploitation by nationalistic demagogues. This very exploitation was the subject of Lehnhoff's carefully planned production, set in a modern country where a military crisis has led to the collapse of parliamentary democracy and the imposition of a totalitarian state. Lohengrin himself, a distasteful playboy in an off-white suit, served as the agent for this change. It was a fascinating interpretation, centering on both the political and popular cultural manifestations of incipient dictatorship. The production, however, often proceeded in direct contradiction to the music, which is some of the most romantic Wagner ever wrote; the bridal chorus, for example, was severely curtailed and represented on the stage by Lohengrin playing seductively on the piano. This flagrant breach between the stage and the orchestra pit, which was far from being to the taste of all members of the audience, made the performance more an exercise in historical criticism than a creative representation.

The gains achieved by the more radical directors of the contemporary stage have perhaps been most apparent in a new production of *The Ring* staged using the combined resources of the *Oper am Rhein*. The adaptable though monumental single set by Andreas Reinhardt emphasized the concentration of Wagner's drama, while setting the production in the nineteenth century related it specifically to the economics of the time and the political conflicts that emerged from them. The family tensions between gods and humans that generate much of the action of the drama were firmly grounded in the commercial and industrial upper class of Victorian society. At the same time, the stage director, Kurt Horres, did not hestiate to engage in flagrant anachronism when the action required it. Thus, the Valkyries, clad in burnished steel from which the stage lights were blindingly reflected, appeared to come from another world but at

the same time served as effective metaphors for the violent forces un-
leashed in the drama. More simply, when the Gibichungs gathered to
welcome Brünnhilde and Gunther to their hall, they were not primitive
tribesmen in skins but top-hatted shareholders carrying rifles, anticipating
a strike in the factory. In the same scene, Hagen flourishing his spear, as
an allusion to more traditional presentations of *The Ring*, acquired a
menacing and disquieting presence. Above all, the certainty of the direction, the accuracy with which each line was delivered and conveyed with
corresponding facial and bodily movements, enabled one to follow the
action with the closeness normally associated with the spoken rather than
the musical theatre. The grand gestures of the nineteenth-century theatre,
which result inevitably from the massive effort required to sing Wagner's
music, appeared entirely natural expressions of the words and music.
Consequently, the drama unfolded with an iron compulsion. For all the
apparent divergence from the details of the original stage directions, the
old master would have recognized in this production a cogent binding of
poetry, music, gesture, and staging that was for him the essence of total
theatre.

NOTES

1. *Baudelaire as a Literary Critic*, ed. & trans. Lois Boe and Francis E. Hyslop, Jr.
(University Park: Pennsylvania State University Press, 1964), 192–193.

2. Herbert Lindenberger, *Opera: The Extravagant Art* (Ithaca: Cornell University
Press, 1984), 285.

3. Mosco Carner, *Puccini* (New York: Knopf, 1959), 159.

4. Raymond Furness, *Wagner and Literature* (New York: St. Martin's Press, 1982),
22–23.

5. Michael P. Steinberg, *The Meaning of the Salzburg Festival: Austria as Theater
and Ideology, 1890–1938* (Ithaca: Cornell University Press, 1990), 25–36.

6. Spike Hughes, *Glyndebourne: A History of the Festival Opera* (Newton Abbot:
David & Charles, 1981), 28.

7. Sally Beauman, *The Royal Shakespeare Company* (Oxford: Oxford University
Press, 1982), 8–67.

8. James W. Flannery, *W. B. Yeats and the Idea of a Theatre* (Toronto: Macmillan,
1976), 102–109.

9. Richard Beacham, *Adolphe Appia* (Cambridge: Cambridge University Press,
1987), 89–97.

10. Penelope Turing, *New Bayreuth* (St. Martin, Jersey, Channel Islands: Jersey
Artists, 1969), 6.

11. Dietrich Mack, *Theaterarbeit an Wagners Ring* (Munich: Piper, 1978), 28.

Chronology of Wagner's Life

Date	Events in Wagner's Life	Theatre and Opera	Public Life
1813	• May 22. Born in Leipzig		• Defeat of Napoleon, Battle of Leipzig
1814		• Debut of actor Edmund Kean in London	• Napoleon banished to Elba
		• Death of actor August Wilhelm Iffland	• Congress of Vienna
		• Ludwig von Beethoven: *Fidelio*	
1815		• Debut of Ludwig Devrient in Berlin	• Return of Napoleon, Battle of Waterloo
1819			• Karlsbad Decrees
1821		• Franz Grillparzer: *The Golden Fleece*	• Death of Napoleon
		• C. M. von Weber: *Der Freischütz*	
1822	• December 2. Enrolls at Dresden Kreuzschule, to Dec. 1827		
1823		• Weber: *Euryanthe*	
1825		• Aleksander Pushkin: *Boris Godunov*	• Decembrist revolt, Russia
1826		• Weber: *Oberon*	

Date	Events in Wagner's Life	Theatre and Opera	Public Life
1827		• Death of Beethoven	
1828	• January 28. Enrolls at Leipzig Nikolaischule	• Daniel Auber: *The Mute Girl of Portici*	
	• Completes *Leubald and Adelaide*	• Ferdinand Raimund: *The King of the Alps and the Misanthrope*	
1829	• April. Sees Wilhelmine Schröder-Devrient in *Fidelio*	• Gioacchino Rossini's last opera: *Guillaume Tell*	
1830	• Easter. Leaves Nikolaischule	• Victor Hugo: *Hernani*	• Revolution in Paris
	• December 25. First music, "Drumbeat Overture," performed in public		
1831	• February. Enrolls at Leipzig University	• Vincenzo Bellini: *Norma*	• Polish uprising suppressed by Russians
		• Giacomo Meyerbeer: *Robert the Devil*	
1832	• Travels to Brünn, Vienna, Prague	• Death of Johann Wolfgang von Goethe	
1833	• Spends year in Würzburg		• German Customs Union
1834	• January 6. Completes *The Fairies*		
	• June. Publishes first essay, "On German Opera"		
	• August 1. Hired as musical director of Bethmann troupe. Meets Minna		
1835		• Gaetano Donizetti: *Lucia di Lammermoor*	
		• Fromental Halévy: *The Jewess*	
1836	• March 29. Première of *The Ban on Love*		• Chartist disturbances in Great Britain
	• July 7. Joins Minna in Königsberg		
	• November 24. Marries Minna		

Date	Events in Wagner's Life	Theatre and Opera	Public Life
1837	• August 21. Appointed music director in Riga	• Death of playwright Georg Büchner	
1838		• Hugo: *Ruy Blas*	
1839	• Summer. Journey from Riga to Paris • Residence in Paris		
1840	• November 10. Completes *Rienzi*	• Friedrich Hebbel: *Judith* • Johann Nestroy: *The Talisman*	
1841	• November. Completes *The Flying Dutchman*		
1842	• April. Leaves Paris, takes up residence in Dresden • October 20. Première of *Rienzi*, Dresden	• Eugène Scribe: *A Glass of Water*	
1843	• January 2. Première of *The Flying Dutchman*, Dresden • February 2. Appointed Kapellmeister, Dresden	• Ludwig Tieck's production of *A Midsummer Night's Dream* in Berlin	
1844		• Giuseppe Verdi: *Ernani*	
1845	• October 19. Première of *Tannhäuser*, Dresden		
1846	• Submits plan to reorganize Dresden Court orchestra		
1847	• Conducts C. W. von Gluck's *Iphigenia in Aulis*	• Verdi: *Macbeth*	
1848	• April 28. Completes *Lohengrin* • Becomes involved with revolutionary groups in Dresden and Vienna • October. Begins work on poem of *Siegfried's Death* (start of work on *The Ring*)		• Revolutions in Paris, Vienna, Venice, Berlin, Milan, and Parma

Date	Events in Wagner's Life	Theatre and Opera	Public Life
1849	• May. Goes into exile in Switzerland as result of involvement in Dresden revolution	• Scribe: *Adrienne Lecouvreur*	• Revolutions in Dresden and Baden
	• Fall. Publishes "Art and Revolution"	• Meyerbeer: *The Prophet*	
	• December. Publishes "The Art-Work of the Future"		
1850	• Spring. "Affair" with Jessie Laussot	• Ivan Turgenev: *A Month in the Country*	
	• August 28. Première of *Lohengrin*, Weimar		
1851	• January 10. Completes *Opera and Drama*	• Verdi: *Rigoletto*	
	• Publishes "A Theatre for Zurich"		
1852	• February. First meeting with Otto and Mathilde Wesendonk	• Alexandre Dumas *fils: The Lady of the Camellias*	
1853	• February. Poems for *The Ring* completed	• Verdi: *Il Trovatore (The Troubador)* and *La traviata (The Woman Who Strayed)*	• Start of Crimean War
	• November. Begins composition of *The Rhinegold*		
1854	• First reads work of Arthur Schopenhauer		
1855	• March-June. Concerts in London		
1856	• October-November. Franz Liszt visits in Zurich		
1857	• Suspends composition of *The Ring* at end of act 2 of *Siegfried*. Begins work on *Tristan and Isolde*		• Indian Mutiny • Emancipation of serfs in Russia
1858	• August. Wagners separate and leave Zurich, Minna going to Dresden, Wagner to Venice	• Jacques Offenbach: *Orpheus in the Underworld*	

Date	Events in Wagner's Life	Theatre and Opera	Public Life
1859	• March. Leaves Venice on expulsion order and settles in Lucerne	• Charles Gounod: *Faust*	• Franco-Austrian War
	• August. Completes composition of *Tristan and Isolde* in Lucerne. Leaves for Paris, where joined by Minna	• Verdi: *A Masked Ball*	• Formation of German National Association to unify Germany under Prussia
1860	• Winter. Concerts in Paris and Brussels	• Aleksander Ostrovski: *The Storm*	
	• Summer. First visit to Germany in eleven years		
1861	• March. Three performances of *Tannhäuser*, Paris Opéra	• Death of Scribe	• Outbreak of U.S. Civil War
	• Travels between Vienna, Mainz, and Paris		
1862	• February. Settles briefly in Biebrich	• Verdi: *La Forza del Destino (The Force of Destiny)*	• Bismarck becomes prime minister of Prussia
	• Bohemian summer	• Death of Nestroy	
	• Unconditional amnesty granted, last meeting with Minna, in Dresden	• Debut of Sarah Bernhardt at Comédie-Française	
1863	• Tours Central Europe and Russia as conductor with home base in Vienna	• Hector Berlioz: *The Trojans*	
1864	• March 23. Leaves Vienna because of debt	• Offenbach: *La Belle Hélène*	
	• May. Summoned to Munich by Ludwig II	• Death of Meyerbeer	
	• June. Beginning of liaison with Cosima von Bülow		
1865	• June 10. First performance of *Tristan and Isolde* in Munich	• Meyerbeer: *The African Girl* (posthumous)	• Assassination of Abraham Lincoln
	• December 10. Leaves Munich as result of political controversy		• U.S. Congress abolishes slavery

Date	Events in Wagner's Life	Theatre and Opera	Public Life
1866	• January 25. Death of Minna	• Henrik Ibsen: *Brand*	• Austro-Italian War
	• April. Moves into Tribschen	• Debut of actor Henry Irving	
1867	• Fall. Publishes articles on "German Art and German Politics"	• Ibsen: *Peer Gynt* • Verdi: *Don Carlo*	• Creation of Hapsburg dual monarchy
1868	• June 21. Première of *The Mastersingers* in Munich	• Death of Rossini	
	• November. First meeting with Friedrich Nietzsche, in Leipzig		
1869	• March 1. Resumes work on *The Ring* after twelve years		
	• May. Elected member of Royal Academy of Arts, Berlin		
	• September. Première of *The Rheingold* in Munich, Wagner not present		
1870	• June 26. Première of *The Valkyrie* in Munich, Wagner not present		• Franco-Prussian War. Siege of Paris
	• August 25. Marriage with Cosima in Lucerne		• Unification of Italy
1871	• Spring. First visit to Bayreuth, determines to settle there	• Verdi: *Aïda*	• Wilhelm I declared German Kaiser at Versailles
	• Treated as celebrity in visits to Leipzig and Berlin		
	• Announces plans for Bayreuth Festival		
1872	• April 22. Moves from Tribschen to Bayreuth	• Debut of Eleanora Duse	
	• May 22. Laying of foundation stone of Festival Theatre		

Date	Events in Wagner's Life	Theatre and Opera	Public Life
1873	• Preparations for Bayreuth Festival		
1874	• April 28. Moves into Wahnfried	• Modest Mussorgski: *Boris Godunov*	
	• November 21. Completes composition of *The Ring*, twenty-one years after beginning music, twenty-five years after beginning poem	• Johann Strauss: *Die Fledermaus* • Debut of Meininger in Berlin	
1875	• Summer. Rehearsals for *The Ring* at Bayreuth	• Georges Bizet: *Carmen*	
1876	• August. First Bayreuth Festival, with first complete performance of *The Ring* • September-December. Holiday in Italy	• Amilcare Ponchielli: *La gioconda*	
1877	• May. Concerts in London to raise money for Bayreuth	• Ibsen: *Pillars of Society*	
1878	• February. First issue of *Bayreuther Blätter* • April. Angelo Neumann stages *The Ring* in Leipzig	• W. S. Gilbert & A. S. Sullivan: *H.M.S. Pinafore*	• Anti-socialist laws passed in Germany
1879	• December 31. Leaves Bayreuth for extended stay in Italy	• Ibsen: *A Doll's House* • P. I. Tchaikovsky: *Eugene Onegin*	
1880	• In Italy most of year	• Gilbert & Sullivan: *The Pirates of Penzance*	
1881	• April. Attends performance of *The Ring* in Berlin	• Ibsen: *Ghosts* • Offenbach: *The Tales of Hoffmann*	
1882	• July 26. Première of *Parsifal* at Bayreuth	• Ibsen: *An Enemy of the People*	
1883	• February 13. Dies in Venice	• Founding of Deutsches Theater, Berlin	

Further Reading

PRIMARY SOURCES

German

Wagner, Cosima. *Tagebücher* (*Diaries*). Edited by Martin Gregor-Dellin and Dietrich Mack. 2 vols. Munich and Zürich: Piper, 1976.

Wagner, Richard. *Gesammelte Schriften und Briefe* (Collected writings and letters). Edited by Julius Kapp. 14 vols. Leipzig: Hesse and Becker, n.d. [1914].

——— . *Mein Leben* (My life). 2d ed. Munich: Bruckmann, 1915.

——— . *Sämtliche Briefe* (Complete letters). Edited by Gertrud Strobel and Werner Wolf. 8 vols. [to date]. Leipzig: Deutscher Verlag für Musik, 1967.

English

Wagner, Cosima. *Diaries*. Translated by Geoffrey Skelton. 2 vols. New York & London: Harcourt, 1977 & 1980.

Wagner, Richard. *The Diary of Richard Wagner, 1865–1882: The Brown Book*. Edited by Joachim Bergfeld, translated by George Bird. Cambridge: Cambridge University Press, 1980.

——— . *My Life*. Translated by Andrew Gray, edited by Mary Whittall. Cambridge: Cambridge University Press, 1983.

——— . *Richard Wagner: Stories & Essays*. Edited by Charles Osborne. London: Owen, 1973.

——— . *Richard Wagner's Prose Works*. Translated by William Ashton Ellis. 8 vols. London: 1892–1899. Reprint New York: Broude, 1966.

——— . *Selected Letters of Richard Wagner*. Edited and translated by Stewart Spencer and Barry Millington. London: Dent, 1987.

———— . *Three Wagner Essays.* Translated by Robert Jacobs. London: Eulenberg, 1979.
———— . *Wagner on Music and Drama: A Compendium of Richard Wagner's Prose Works.* Edited by Albert Goldman and Evert Sprinchorn. New York: Da Capo, 1964.
———— . *Wagner Writes from Paris.* Edited and translated by Robert Jacobs and Geoffrey Skelton. New York: J. Day, 1973.

BIOGRAPHY

Barth, Herbert, Dietrich Mack, and Egon Voss, eds. *Wagner: A Documentary Study.* London: Thames & Hudson, 1975.
Chamberlain, Houston Stewart. *Richard Wagner.* Philadelphia: Lippencott, 1897.
Chancellor, John. *Wagner.* Boston: Little, Brown, 1978.
Gregor-Dellin, Martin. *Richard Wagner: His Life, His Work, His Century.* Translated by J. Maxwell Brownjohn. San Diego: Harcourt, 1983.
Gutman, Robert. *Richard Wagner: The Man, His Mind, and His Music.* New York: Harcourt, 1968.
James, Burnett. *Wagner and the Romantic Disaster.* New York: Midas Hippocrene, 1983.
Millington, Barry. *Wagner.* The Master Musicians. London: Dent, 1986.
Newman, Ernest. *The Life of Richard Wagner.* 4 vols. New York: Knopf, 1933–1946.
———— . *Wagner as Man and Artist.* New York: Knopf, 1924.
Nietzsche, Friedrich. "Richard Wagner in Bayreuth," *Untimely Meditations.* Trans. R. J. Hollingdale. Intro. J. P. Stern. Cambridge: Cambridge University Press, 1983.
Skelton, Geoffrey. *Richard and Cosima Wagner: Biography of A Marriage.* Boston: Houghton Mifflin, 1982.
Taylor, Ronald. *Richard Wagner: His Life, Art and Thought.* New York: Taplinger, 1979.
Wapnewski, Peter. *Der traurige Gott: Richard Wagner in seinen Helden.* Munich: Beck, 1978.
Watson, Derek. *Richard Wagner: A Biography.* London: Dent, 1979.
Westernhagen, Curt von. *Wagner: A Biography.* 2 vols. Cambridge: Cambridge University Press, 1978.

STAGE HISTORY

Appia, Adolphe. *Staging Wagnerian Drama.* Translated by Peter Loeffler. Basel: Birkhäuser, 1982.
Bauer, Oswald Georg. *Richard Wagner: The Stage Designs and Productions from the Premières to the Present.* New York: Rizzoli, 1983.
Beacham, Richard. *Adolphe Appia: Theatre Artist.* Cambridge: Cambridge University Press, 1987.
Cook, Peter. *A Memoir of Bayreuth, 1876.* London: 1979.
Hartford, Robert, ed. *Bayreuth: The Early Years.* Cambridge: Cambridge University Press, 1980.
Mack, Dietrich, ed. *Der Bayreuther Inszenierungstil.* Munich: Prestel, 1976.
———— , ed. *Theaterarbeit an Wagners Ring.* Munich: Piper, 1978.
Petzet, Detta, and Michael Petzet. *Die Richard Wagner-Bühne König Ludwigs II.* Munich: Prestel, 1970.

Porges, Heinrich. *Wagner Rehearsing the Ring: An Eye-Witness Account of the Stage Rehearsals of the First Bayreuth Festival.* Translated by Robert L. Jacobs. Cambridge: Cambridge University Press, 1983.

Skelton, Geoffrey. *Wagner at Bayreuth: Experiment and Tradition.* London: Barrie & Rockliff, 1965.

Srocke, Martina. *Richard Wagner als Regisseur.* Berliner Musikwissenschaftliche Arbeiten. Munich: Katzbichler, 1988.

Turing, Penelope. *New Bayreuth.* St. Martin, Jersey, Channel Islands: Jersey Artists, 1969.

CRITICAL

General Works

Adorno, Theodor. *In Search of Wagner.* Translated by Rodney Livingstone. London: NLB, 1981.

Amerongen, Martin van. *Wagner: A Case History.* Translated by Stewart Spencer and Dominic Cakebread. New York: Braziller, 1984.

Barzun, Jacques. *Darwin, Marx, Wagner: Critique of a Heritage.* 2d ed. Garden City, New York: Doubleday, 1958.

Bekker, Paul. *Richard Wagner: His Life in His Work.* Translated by M. M. Bozeman. Freeport, New York: Books for Libraries, 1931.

Borchmeyer, Dieter. *Richard Wagner: Theory and Theatre.* Translated by Stewart Spencer. Oxford: Clarendon Press, 1991.

Burbidge, Peter, and Richard Sutton. *The Wagner Companion.* New York: Cambridge University Press, 1979.

Dahlhaus, Carl. *Richard Wagner's Music Dramas.* Translated by Mary Whittall. Cambridge: Cambridge University Press, 1980.

Deathridge, John, and Carl Dahlhaus. *The New Grove Wagner.* The Composer Biography Series. New York: Norton, 1984.

Garten, H. F. *Wagner the Dramatist.* London: Calder, 1977.

Kunze, S., ed. *Richard Wagner: von der Oper zum Musikdrama.* Berne and Munich: Francke, 1978.

Laudon, Robert T. *Sources of the Wagnerian Synthesis.* Musikwissenschaftliche Schriften. Salzburg: Katzbichler, 1979.

Magee, Bryan. *Aspects of Wagner.* Revised and enlarged. Oxford: Oxford University Press, 1988.

Millington, Barry, ed. *The Wagner Compendium: A Guide to Wagner's Life and Music.* London: Thames & Hudson, 1992.

Millington, Barry, and Stewart Spencer, eds. *Wagner in Performance.* Yale University Press, 1992.

Müller, Ulrich, and Peter Wapnewski, eds. *Richard-Wagner Handbuch.* Stuttgart: Kröner, 1986.

———. *The Wagner Handbook.* Translated and edited by John Deathridge. Cambridge, MA: Harvard University Press, 1992.

Newman, Ernest. *The Wagner Operas.* New York: Knopf, 1949.

Skelton, Geoffrey. *Wagner in Thought and Practice.* London: Lime Tree, 1991.

Stein, Jack. *Richard Wagner and the Synthesis of the Arts*. Detroit: Wayne State University Press, 1960.
Tanner, Michael. "The Total Work of Art." In *The Wagner Companion*, edited by Peter Burbridge and Richard Sutton. New York: Cambridge University Press, 1979.

Individual Works

The Flying Dutchman

Csampai, Attila, and Dietmar Holland. *Der fliegende Holländer: Texte, Materialien, Kommentare*. Hamburg: Ricordi, 1982.
John, Nicholas, ed. *Der fliegende Holländer*. Opera Guides 12. New York: Riverrun, 1982.
Pahlen, Kurt. *Richard Wagner: Der fliegende Holländer*. Munich: Goldmann, 1979.

The Mastersingers of Nuremberg

John, Nicholas, ed. *Die Meistersinger von Nürnberg*. New York: Riverrun, 1983.
Pahlen, Kurt, ed. *Die Meistersinger von Nürnberg*. Munich: Goldmann, 1981.

Parsifal

Beckett, Lucy. *Richard Wagner: Parsifal*. Cambridge: Cambridge University Press, 1981.

Rienzi

Deathridge, John. *Wagner's Rienzi: A Reappraisal Based on a Study of the Sketches and Drafts*. Oxford: Clarendon Press, 1977.

The Ring of the Nibelung

Cooke, Deryck. *I Saw the World End: A Study of Wagner's Ring*. London: Oxford University Press, 1979.
Corse, Sandra. *Wagner and the New Consciousness: Language and Love in the Ring*. London: Associated University Press, 1990.
DiGaetani, John Louis, ed. *Penetrating Wagner's Ring: An Anthology*. New York: Da Capo, 1983.
Donington, Robert. *Wagner's Ring and Its Symbols*. London: Faber & Faber, 1963.
John, Nicholas, ed. *The Rhinegold/Das Rheingold*. New York: Riverrun, 1985.
———. *Siegfried*. New York: Riverrun, 1984.
———. *Twilight of the Gods/Götterdämmerung*. New York: Riverrun, 1985.
———. *The Valkyrie/Die Walküre*. New York: Riverrun, 1983.
McCreless, Patrick. *Wagner's Siegfried: Its Drama, History and Music*. Ann Arbor: UMI Research Press: 1982.
Rather, L. J. *The Dream of Self-Destruction: Wagner's Ring and the Modern World*. Baton Rouge: Louisiana State University Press, 1979.
Shaw, George Bernard. *The Perfect Wagnerite: Major Critical Essays*. Edited by Michael Holroyd. Harmondsworth: Penguin, 1986.

Tannhäuser

Csampai, Attila, and Dietmar Holland. *Tannhäuser, Texte, Materialien, Kommentare*.
Hamburg: Ricordi, 1986.
John, Nicholas, ed. *Tannhäuser*. New York: Riverrun, 1988.

Tristan and Isolde

John, Nicholas, ed. *Tristan and Isolde*. New York: Riverrun, 1981.
Zuckerman, Elliott. *The First Hundred Years of Wagner's Tristan*. New York: Columbia
University Press, 1964.

Wagner's Influence

Furness, Raymond. *Wagner and Literature*. New York: St. Martin's Press, 1982.
Large, David C., and William Weber. *Wagnerism in European Culture and Politics*.
Ithaca, NY: Cornell University Press, 1984.

Index

About the Author

SIMON WILLIAMS is Professor of Dramatic Art and Director of the Interdisciplinary Humanities Center at the University of California, Santa Barbara. He is the author of *German Actors of the Eighteenth and Nineteenth Centuries* (Greenwood, 1985) and *Shakespeare on the German Stage.*